Applied Leadership

Applied Leadership

Developing Stages for Creating Exceptional Leaders

Sam Altawil

BEP

BUSINESS EXPERT PRESS

Leader in applied, concise business books

First published in 2023 by
Business Expert Press, LLC
222 East 46th Street, New York, NY 10017
www.businessexpertpress.com

ISBN-13: 978-1-63742-561-9 (paperback)
ISBN-13: 978-1-63742-562-6 (e-book)

Business Expert Press Human Resource Management and Organizational Behavior Collection

First edition: 2023

10 9 8 7 6 5 4 3 2 1

Thank you to my family and friends for the support.
Thank you, Ryan Soehn, for your assistance.

Description

Applied Leadership: Developing Stages for Creating Exceptional Leaders is a comprehensive, self-development practical leadership book. Designed to be a complete self-training guide for individuals in all stages of leadership, from entry level to advance stages.

For years, organizations and individuals have struggled with ineffective leadership training. It neither served to strengthen the current leaders in the organization nor created future leaders for that organization, until NOW. Because great leadership is an evolutionary process, this publication will offer the reader a journey to become an exceptional leader. Individuals will be able to develop the practical skills necessary to be excellent leaders for any organization.

No longer will organizations outsource costly training sessions that last for weeks or months for their staff, rather, this book will provide those necessary steps, skills, and knowledge needed at their own pace.

Keywords

what are the stages for business leadership development?; how to develop fundamental business leadership training?; what are the stages for creating exceptional business leaders?; what is the evolution of leadership in business?; how to develop practical leadership skills in business?; what is the journey of leadership in business?; how do I self-develop leadership skills?; what is self-development leadership training?; how to create exceptional business leaders?; how to develop business managers?; what are the leadership development stages?; how to apply leadership training to practical use?; is there a practical business leadership development?; is there a comprehensive business leadership training?; how to develop emotional intelligence for leaders?; how do leaders motivate their staff?; how to develop soft/human skills for leaders in business?; how to develop communication skills for leaders in business?; how do business leaders motivate their employees?; are ethics included in business leadership training?

Contents

PHASE 1
The Initial Step

CHAPTER 1

Introduction Into Leadership

Imagine a workplace where the leaders in the organization, from supervisors to CEO, have high regard from their staff. Imagine these leaders leading by example, influencing and empowering their staff, rather than leading by authority, tyranny, micromanagement, and fear. Imagine an organization not only promotes discussion but actually listens to their employees. Imagine an organization that utilizes their employee's ideas and properly rewards them for it. Imagine an organization that has little management–employee relations conflicts. Imagine an organization providing job security for their employees. Imagine a culture in which employees publicly endorse the organization.

Depending on each individual's perspective and experience, one might find this workplace imagination unimaginative, given the fact that many estimate the majority of organizations fail in one or more areas listed above. Though, those same individuals will likely recognize that with great leadership, the probability of achieving a great place to work and a successful organization will likely be very high. Fortunately, there are, and have been organizations which have achieved all around success, both internally with their employees and externally with their clients and marketplace. Many attribute this success to good leadership and simply believe that good leaders elevate people to organizational success, while bad leaders do the opposite. Yet, throughout time, we have seen, or even heard of bad leaders achieving the same organizational success as good leaders, but is this factual? And is it really possible?

There are many questions that encompass the topic of leadership, and most have discovered there were no obvious answers to any of them. Some answers are based on research, direct work experience, and, on some occasions, speculation. Leadership is not an exact science, nor an exact social science. There are different styles of leadership with distinct personalities, leading different types of employees, such as laborers, professionals, and management. Nevertheless, we do recognize that leadership is part of organizational structures and vital in the workplace.

As with everything in life, leadership must have a beginning, a journey, and an ending. The beginning is the most critical stage for any upcoming leader for several reasons: First, as a person becomes a new supervisor, manager, or any other leader in the organization, he or she will be challenged with how to lead, set goals, evaluate, communicate and direct staff, and so forth. Without prior training, this new leader will be managing by trial and error which will ultimately have negative results with possibly long-term consequences. Such as, if failure is significant, it might dishearten the new leader to resign, and he or she might never have the opportunity to fulfill their full professional potential. Other likely harm might occur to the organization, department, or staff, depending on the leadership role of this new leader.

Second, in this beginning stage, it is essential to learn and develop the core competencies of leadership, which I will discuss in more detail in Phase 2. And third, adapting to those core competencies and being mindful in its application during the learning process.

Still, no learning process is complete without some historical understanding of the topic. Leadership is a timeless and multicultural subject that has been discussed for thousands of years and will continue for thousands more. Its evolutionary development has helped shape and redefine our thoughts about workforce management in all organizations.

CHAPTER 2

Brief History of Leadership Theories

It is believed by some historians that the first writing on the subject of leadership was by the Egyptians in the form of hieroglyphics, dating back almost 5,000 years (Grace 2003). However, this should not surprise anyone, given the fact that mankind always had singular individuals who led others, regardless of the task at hand. By nature, human beings are social and tribal creatures, and as such, their group behavior structure is that of leaders and followers. Yet, throughout the years, scholars, historians, philosophers, and others began examining leadership closely and developed different theories, which are still being studied today. Some of these impactful theories include the following.

Great Man Theory (1795–1881)

The Great Man Theory, sometimes called the Trait Theory, can be traced back to Thomas Carlyle and Francis Galton (1822–1911). This theory was first introduced by historian Thomas Carlyle, who once remarked on the great men or heroes in history by stating "the history of the world is but the biography of great men" (Carlyle 1869). Reinforcing this thinking, in the mid-1800s, Francis Galton (cousin of Charles Darwin), in his publication, supported the idea that some individuals are naturally born to lead (Galton 1891). Such individuals have distinctive traits and skills that make them great, and these things cannot be taught or learned. In other words, a leader with the noble qualities of a hero. While Thomas Carlyle was credited for the Great Man Theory years before, individuals such as Plato, Aristotle, and Niccolò Machiavelli shared the main ideas of this theory before it was established (Henman 2011).

Many have criticized this theory as being presumptuous in two main areas: one, being exclusive for only recognizing men's leadership accomplishments, and fails to recognize that throughout history, there have been many female leaders who achieved success during their time.

Two, the notion of leaders who are born and cannot be developed is viewed from a narrow lens of historically accomplished leaders. Perhaps the definition of leadership in the Great Man Theory is primarily for those who are leaders of countries, such as kings, presidents, and so forth. Of course, there are leaders beyond just kings and presidents in this world, and in later times, most scholars have recognized leaders from different entities, such as militaries, worship organizations, businesses, and more. Some of those scholars began examining successful leaders and their commonalities, from personalities to behaviors, which led to the next development of Trait Leadership theory.

Trait Theory (1904–1974)

Trait theory focuses on identifying various personality traits and characteristics that are associated with successful leadership in different circumstances. Yet, in the later 20th century, trait research continued with Ralph Stogdill, who challenged the traditional trait-based theory (Stogdill 1948). Ralph Stogdill was a professor emeritus of Management Science and Psychology at Ohio State University and was internationally known for his research and publications on leadership and organizations. He was a fellow of both the American Psychological Association and the Academy of Management.

In Ralph Stogdill's first survey, he analyzed and combined more than 124 traits studied between 1904 and 1947 (Northouse 2021). After a full analysis, he identified eight traits that related to how individuals in different groups become leaders. His results showed that the average person's traits in a leadership role are different from the average group member. Ralph Stogdill finalized these traits as follows: *Intelligence, insight, responsibility, alertness, confidence, initiative, persistence*, and *sociability*. However, a person does not become a leader solely because he or she has these traits; in fact, Ralph Stogdill determined that such a leader's traits must be relevant to the situation in which the leader is operating.

In other words, a leader in one situation does not make him or her a leader in another situation.

In his second survey, Ralph Stogdill analyzed another 163 studies that he completed between 1948 and 1970 (Northouse 2021). Though, this time, his findings changed from his first survey results. After further examination of the 163 studies, he concluded that situational factors coupled with skill and behavior traits are determinant factors for leadership. Similar to his first survey, Ralph Stogdill included 10 additional behavior and skill traits that encompass motivation and competencies, ranging from being influential, driven to willingness, and goal-oriented. While many associate Ralph Stogdill with trait theory, others believe that he gave rise to behavior approach to leadership studies.

Behavior Theory (1950–1970)

The fundamental difference between Trait Leadership and Behavior Leadership theories is that Trait Leadership presumes only certain people are born with the qualities and characteristics of good leadership, and individuals cannot be taught these traits. However, Behavior Leadership focuses on the actions of a leader rather than inherent traits. Through teaching and observation, one can become a leader, as long as he or she acquires the necessary skills and behavior of a good leader. Many have contributed to this study (Blake et al. 1964; MacGregor 1960; Katz and Kahn 1978; Stogdill and Coons 1957).

This theory focuses on observing the patterns of effective leadership behaviors, and it was identified that there are different styles of leadership behaviors that are functional. This includes Task-oriented leaders, Relationship-oriented leaders, Status-quo leaders, Dictatorial leaders, and more. Though, most have focused on the dichotomy between Task-oriented versus Relationship-oriented leadership styles, especially in modern times. Both play an important role in leadership, but with a different approach. Generally speaking, a Task-oriented leader is motivated by completing projects, which requires setting goals, planning, defining roles and responsibilities, and evaluating performances. One can say, this style of a leader makes an excellent project manager. On the other hand, behavior-oriented leader is motivated by developing relationships with their staff, empowering them to excel, building a supportive work environment, and so on. Both are effective in different circumstances.

Like other leadership theories, behavior theory leadership has many advantages; it does not exclude anyone from their desire to become a leader. It allows individuals to choose the style of leadership that best suits their situation, and it allows the flexibility for leaders to implement the actions of their choice. Still, there are some disadvantages; with the flexibility to make choices, this theory does not directly suggest a choice or choices in certain circumstances. It presumes each individual will make the right choice of leadership styles in different situations, even though individuals have different values, backgrounds, motives, and so on. Which, in most occasions, contributes to their decision-making process. Then again, most will agree that the advantages outweigh the disadvantages, especially since the Behavior Leadership study gave rise to other leadership studies throughout the years.

Contingency Theory (1967–1990)

Since the 1950s, researchers focused on isolating effective leadership behavior, which gave rise to the contingency leadership theory. Contingency theory approach contends that a leader's success depends on whether the style of his or her leadership is suited for a particular situation. For example, if placing a particular business leader in a nonbusiness situation, in which his or her leadership style matches the situation, this business leader will most likely succeed.

In the 1960s, Fred Fiedler, a leading researcher of organizational psychology in the 20th century, developed the first theory utilizing the contingency approach (Fiedler 1964). His focus was leadership effectiveness with group performance. After examining the personalities and characteristics of leaders, Fred Fiedler focused on three extensive classifications: Leadership Style, Situational Control, and Matching Styles to the Situation.

1. *Leadership Style*: According to Fred Fiedler, leadership styles are fixed based on the leader's background, values, and overall life experience and, therefore, cannot be changed (Fiedler 1964). For this

reason, he developed a measuring matrix called the Least Preferred Co-worker (LPC). The LPC scale determines whether the leader's style is Relationship-oriented or Task-oriented by measuring his or her least preferred co-worker from one to eight rating. A high score rating of a co-worker indicates a more positive view of the least preferred co-worker, while a low score rating indicates the opposite. This rating is based on interpersonal components such as warmth, sincerity, cold, kind, polite, unfriendly, and so on. Individuals with a high LPC score are motivated to maintain congenial interpersonal relationships, whereas individuals with a low LPC score are motivated on task achievements. Once, a Task-oriented or Relationship-oriented style of leadership is established, it now can be matched to the proper situation to optimize the possibility of group results.

2. *Situational Control*: Fred Fiedler maintains, that the more control leaders have over their work environment and staff, the more likely such leaders will be effective in achieving their goals. Situational control refers to favorable work settings for leaders, but only if they maintain good working relations with their staff. Assign clear tasks in accordance to each staff's abilities. Utilize his or her authority to better develop the team, and be equitable in terms of rewards and punishments.

3. *Matching Styles to the Situations*: Fred Fiedler believed that each of the two styles (Task-oriented and Relationship-oriented) must match their appropriate situations in order to be effective. He believes that these traits are stable traits which are not easily adaptable to change, and therefore any attempt to encourage these styles to adjust to unfitting situations will be very difficult. Fred Fiedler describes three kinds of situations that Task-oriented and Relationship-oriented can best suit their style: low-control, medium-control, and high-control (Fiedler 1964). Task-oriented tends to be in the high-control, while Relationship-oriented tends to be in the low- to medium-control.

   • Fred Fiedler found there are certain patterns that seem to complement each style. With Task-oriented leadership style, their motive is to get the job done, which requires a work environment and staff driven by the overall same objective of completing projects, overseeing work processes, meeting deadlines, producing products, and so on. For this type of leader, this work environment and staff are consistent and efficient, provided each staff member understands his or her roles and responsibilities. Yet, some have argued this type of work settings leave little room for creativity among the team.

- With Relationship-oriented style, leaders rely on interpersonal skills to motivate, influence, and empower others to maximize group performance. In this work environment, creativity is welcomed and encouraged in efforts to fulfill the overall objectives. These leaders tend to take personal interest in the welfare of their staff, both personal and professional. The results usually, an increase in staff loyalty, respect, and a willingness to do more without being asked. Therefore, these types of leaders can have low-control and still be able to complete tasks.

As with most leadership theories, they have their advantages and disadvantages. Fred Fiedler's theory is very precise and effective in certain circumstances, yet rigid without any room for flexibility. Still, his theory helped launch other series of contingency leadership theory studies.

Situational Leadership Theory (1969–1980)

In 1969, Paul Hersey and Ken Blanchard created the Situational Leaders theory, but at the time they introduced it as the Life Cycle Theory of Leadership (Hersey and Blanchard 1969). Paul Hersey was a behavior scientist and author of several publications, such as *Management of Organization Behavior*, now in its 10th edition. Ken Blanchard was a business consultant, motivational speaker, and author of many books, including *The One Minute Manager*, which was his most successful book at the time.

In Paul Hersey and Ken Blanchard's theory, successful leaders are those who adapt different leadership styles to the situation, group, or individual. Their model has two fundamental concepts. The first is Leadership Style, in which they portray this style as the amount of task-behavior and relationship-behavior that leaders provide. There are four leadership behavior styles described by Paul Hersey and Ken Blanchard: Telling, Selling, Participating, and Delegating.

1. *Telling*: When individuals lack specific skills for the job, the leader "tells" them what and how to do the job.
2. *Selling*: When individuals are able to do the job, yet lack the willingness to do so, the leader "sells" the purpose and the reasoning for doing the tasks.
3. *Participating*: When individuals are able and willing to do the tasks yet lack the confidence to do so, the leader in this situation "participates" beside these individuals to complete the tasks.
4. *Delegating*: When individuals are skilled and confident at completing the tasks, leaders only need to direct them by "delegating" tasks to each one.

The second is Maturity Levels, in which Paul Hersey and Ken Blanchard identify four levels of individual maturity, M1 to M4. M1 being the lowest mature capability, while M4 being the highest mature capability:

1. *M4 Capable*: Experienced and comfortable at task completion.
2. *M3 Capable but Unwilling*: Experienced and comfortable at task completion but lack the confidence or the willingness to take responsibilities.
3. *M2 Unable but Confident*: Able to do the task, yet lacks motivation to do so.
4. *M1 Unable and Insecure*: Inexperienced at completing the task but are willing to learn and work at completing the task.

The advantages of this theory are that it is easy to learn, easy to follow, and practical to use, especially for new managers. Fundamentally, it covers basic management tactics used in various industries today and allows leaders the flexibility to shift styles, when necessary. However, the disadvantages is that it does not seem to be designed for long-term goals. Maturity levels are defined in terms of level of skills and experience, without considering other human factors, such as emotional

intelligence. Lastly, it presumes all leaders have the competency to identify the maturity levels of their followers. Overall, the advantages of this
theory outweigh its disadvantages, in which one can improve it by building upon its foundation.

Transactional Leadership Theory (1947–1981)

Another theory developed in the 20th century called Transactional theory, by a German sociologist by the name of Max Weber in 1947, in
which, later the study continued in 1981 by Bernard Bass (Weber 1947;
Bass 1981). This theory focuses on a leadership style used by most managers, which is authority. It emphasizes on the basic management practice of
supervising processes, staff, and short-term planning. It directs followers
through appealing to their own self-interests.

In this theory, leaders motivate their staff by rewards and punishments. Those who perform their job duties well are rewarded, which most
likely is with monetary resources. Those who perform their job duties
poorly will be subject to disciplinary actions, which could lead to termination. This practice was highly used after World War II and is still being
used today, especially by novice leaders of the organization.

The advantages of this leadership style are that it provides the clear-
cut structure for organizations, helps accomplish short-term objectives,
defines rewards and punishments expectations, and works well with
self-interested employees. However, the disadvantages of this style are
that it lacks the support for creativity, it fails to recognize and reward new
ideas, and monetary rewards are the only choice for good performance.
For most of the leadership theories, the Transactional theory is the least
complex, and for this reason, it is extensively used in today's time. Some
experts believe that but for this theory being rigid, it has the potential to
be developed for more creativity.

Transformational Leadership Theory (1978–1985)

The concept of Transformational leadership was first introduced by James
Burns in 1978 (Burns 1978). James Burns was a political scientist, historian, and authority on leadership studies. He describes Transformational

leadership as leaders and followers assisting each other to progress to a higher level of morale and motivation. Unlike Transactional theory, in which leaders use rewards and punishments to motivate their followers, in Transformational theory, leaders are essentially role models, that are inspiring, motivating, and empowering. These leaders must have a clear understanding of their follower's strengths and weaknesses, in order to align tasks that optimize their performance and develop them to reach their full potential.

Transformational leaders tend to have a proactive approach trait, a desire to improve or change the culture of the organization and influence their staff's personal interest into a team mindset. On the contrary, Transactional leaders tend to be reactive, work within organizational culture, and influence their staff by appealing to their own self-interest.

Some criticized Transformational leadership style as being effectively limited. It thrives on the specific type of employees and their profession or specific type of organizational culture. For example, in organizations that rely on creativity for their success and are generally limited on daily routines, Transformational leaders would succeed, while Transactional leaders would most likely not. However, in a less creative, more routine work environment, by which products are produced in numbers, Transactional leaders thrive in these types of situations.

Final Thought on History of Leadership Theories

These leadership theories are designed to help individuals become great leaders, and each scholar of such theories has extensively researched and developed a process. As noted previously, each leadership theory and process have their own advantages and disadvantages, partly because human behavior that governs leadership is not an exact science, nor general human behavior is a mathematical equation. Another reason is because behavior scientists, historians, and other scholars have developed these theories based on their professional backgrounds. In other words, those who are organizational psychologists might focus primarily on behavior data of leaders and followers, while historians might focus on the past conduct of leaders and followers. Both are valid studies, but both have their advantages and disadvantages.

Thankfully, these scholars have laid the foundation for developing leadership studies and processes, and at the same time, they revealed the importance of leadership development for all organizations. As each generation creates something beneficial for mankind, it is up to the next generation to learn from their accomplishments and attempt to evolve them or create new ones.

PHASE 2

The First Stage—
The Genesis of a Leader

In this publication, the primary focus will be on the individual's journey to leadership, from acquiring the necessary skills that leaders must have, to exploring the different stages and challenges of leadership throughout the life span of her or his career. Individuals will be able to discover their own leadership style, or perhaps formulate their own leadership style, and apply it to their current or future work.

CHAPTER 3

Leadership Has to Have a Beginning

With my first book *On the Edge of Effectiveness*, I introduced a concept for organizations to develop their own leadership training by focusing on four fundamental core competencies (Altawil 2019). It was entitled the Four Fundamental Approach (FFA) to leadership design. This concept originated during my work in the manufacturing industry, in which most of the supervisors, managers, and other leaders were promoted or hired to leadership roles without prior leadership training or extensive experience. Not surprisingly, the outcome of untrained leaders in these roles had negatively impacted the relations between employees and management. Implementing the FFA was concentrated on some elementary management proficiencies, which required: (1) specific human skills, (2) basic business knowledge, (3) strong technical skills, and (4) to be governed by ethical conduct and practices.

Because of the FFA's simplicity, the implementation was successful. These untrained leaders were able to understand the concepts in a relatively short time; simultaneously, they were able to identify their own strengths and areas that needed improvements. While FFA can help organizations develop their own fundamental leadership training, individuals who have a strong desire to become leaders can utilize the FAA as the foundation for their leadership self-development training and allow them to continue to the next stage of leadership self-development.

Developing Core Management Competencies

Arguably, the beginning stage of leadership development is of utmost significance, as it establishes the necessary foundation to progress leaders to the next stage of growth. Individuals must strengthen their technical skills, acquire business knowledge, cultivate their human skills, and apply ethical conduct, as previously described by the FFA.

CHAPTER 4

Technical Skills

Leaders in the workforce are required to have certain technical proficiencies to lead others in the organization, department, and/or teams. These technical proficiencies are necessary to ensure the assigned job(s) are completed properly and also ensure that leaders can teach and develop others in the team and/or the organization.

Generally, technical skills are specialized knowledge and functional understandings of a specific occupation. Occupations such as physicians, electricians, engineers, and more. But technical skills can also be an important requirement of a specific job, such as customer service in retail positions or certain computer knowledge in administrative positions.

For upcoming leaders who decide to pursue leadership, they must take the first step and choose to learn a specific profession, whether it be by formal education, trade school, on-the-job training, books, and/or seminars. Depending on the profession, one can combine college courses with seminars, or trade schools with books and trade publications, and so on.

Yet, for new, or current leaders, who are considering enhancing or developing new skills will require some self-analysis of their own proficiencies. These individuals must evaluate their own technical strengths and areas that need improvements. While, taking into account, that in leadership, even if one does not have expertise and knowledge in every aspect of the profession, he or she must understand the overall concepts of the particular profession.

The main challenge is, as time goes by, most leaders become too busy and, on many occasions, overwhelmed with daily, weekly, and monthly work tasks. The thought of improving or even refreshing one's technical skills never seems to be necessary for leaders, partly because, for some, there is a mindset of "been there, done that," which means they have obtained their knowledge in the past and feel no need to repeat it. Unfortunately, what most leaders do not realize is, if you are not using some or all the technical skills regularly, you will forget some elements of such skills, and in many occasions, these elements are critical.

Still, there are some tactical approaches to enhancing or developing new skills without repeating one's entire educational process, and here are a few suggestions:

- Going back to previous notes or past textbooks and finding key areas might need refreshing—if past notes and textbooks still exist.
- Seminars and/or webinars on key topics, which are designed to update one's current knowledge of certain topics.
- Utilize publication from technical professional sites.
- Utilize or develop a network of professionals and exchange in discussion about topics relating to technical skills and perhaps tactics.
- RESEARCH—utilizing any credible means necessary, including professional Internet sites, public, and/or college libraries.

Lastly, improving technical skills must be considered an ongoing process for leaders. Not only it strengthens one's knowledge to make proper work decisions, but it also assists with training others by designing a one-on-one and group staff development, in addition to creating training manuals for current and future staff.

Not all leaders can teach. In fact, some will argue that most leaders are incapable of teaching or training others for many reasons. The most obvious reason is they do not know how. The other reason is time, simply because most leaders' time is consumed with the daily challenges of their tasks, staff, department, and/or organization. Nonetheless, teaching is a learned skill, and upcoming leaders should take the time and develop this skill.

Creating Training Manuals

Creating *Training Manuals* might be the simplest to learn since it is a process that most can learn to follow. The purpose of the training manual is to ensure consistencies with training and practice. Training manuals are technical documents designed to communicate a standard of practice to be used for the training for a consistent workflow. Most department heads or managers of operations rely heavily on such documents, not only to ensure consistencies but also to avoid recreating operational training time after time.

There are many guides and tools on the Web which can help with developing training manuals, including books and articles, and they can all be helpful. However, before beginning to draft a training manual, assess the training needs and identify the areas, subject matter, or work processes in which training is critical. Subsequently, develop a general timeline and utilize change management strategies. In addition, utilize any tool that might be helpful, whether software, handouts, outlines, presentation boards, and so on. Thereafter, begin outlining the training subject(s) or process from where it begins to where it should end. Once completed, the outline will be used as the table of contents for the training manual.

Outline Sample

- Introducing the training process or topic and set result expectations after completing the training.
- Define and detail the purpose of the training topic or process.
- Begin with the first stage of training, which is the start of the topic or process.
- Continue to the central part of the training (it should be detailed in the outline).
- Conclude with the last stage of the training (it should be detailed in the outline).

Once the training manual is completed, begin to develop summaries of each training subject matter. Essentially, the summaries are general key areas of that subject highlighted, without the details, in the actual training manual. It is designed to be used as a tool to refresh the training without completing the entire training from the beginning. Typically, the refresher summaries should be about a page or two which can be handed to individuals or of course be available electronically.

The main challenge with the summaries is *not* to recreate the training manual by overwriting, but rather prioritizing the subjects and summarizing in an easy outline format. One thought is to use the table of contents of the original training manual as an outline. Thereafter, utilize the key topics and write a brief training refresher. Of course, there is no standard for writing summaries for training, so one can be as creative in various ways.

One-on-One Training

With one-on-one training (which some might refer to as "hands-on" training), a leader is required to show an individual a step-by-step instruction of each task. This process can be time-consuming, but it is very effective because it allows individuals to ask clarifying questions and allows a leader to evaluate the individual's progress to determine if further training is necessary in certain areas. In this type of training settings, a leader must be prepared, patient, communicate clearly, and above all, utilize training manuals, summary manuals, or any other materials that the staff can use to refresh his or her training.

Group Training

For group training, it is less individualized training and more centered on instructing a group collectively. It can comprise presenting materials in either presentation format, such as PowerPoint, or instructing individuals through a step-by-step approach. Depending on the size of the group and the training materials, leaders must make the appropriate judgments as to which is the most practical and effective training approach and setting. Similar to individual training, leaders must create a summary of the training materials to help reinforce the studied materials and allow each individual in the group to have their own copy to reference when needed. Furthermore, leaders should explore other resources for staff training, whether it be topic-specific webinars, outside trainers, consultants, or other online training; though, as long as the leader's technical skills are advanced enough to adequately choose the proper training subjects for his or her staff.

CHAPTER 5

Business Knowledge

Organizational Thinking

In different stages of leadership, there is one critical pitfall which many leaders fall into and that is the inability to think organizationally. Organizationally thinking is a thought process in which leaders consider "what's best" for the organization as a whole, from teamwork with others, and employee engagements, to supporting the short-term and long-term financial stabilities of the organization.

This thought process begins with having a clear understanding of the mission or purpose of the organization, for instance: What does the organization do? Who does it serve? And how does it generate revenue? An organization can be a profit-driven business, government entity, or nonprofit with a mission to serve the community. Next, having a clear understanding of the mechanisms of the organization, which is each internal department simultaneously working together for the purpose of operating the organization. Lastly, having a clear understanding of the importance of the right talent or employee functioning in each of those departments, and their contribution to the success of the organization.

Also, part of thinking organizationally is to understand the business industry in which one is employed, whether high tech, health care, manufacturing, and so on. Each industry has a unique culture and industry standard for conducting business, and for leaders, it is vital to understand the purpose of their industry and how it operates, especially from revenue-generating aspect.

Yet, most leaders (who do not have a master of business administration (MBA) degree) only need to understand some practical business fundamentals, which can include:

- Basic Budgeting
- Forecasting
- Change Management

- Professional Presentation
- Time Management
- Basic Business Management
- Marketing
- Business Ethics
- Basic Business Law

Basic Budgeting

One of the most crucial responsibilities of all leaders is to be financially responsible in all their work activities, from hiring, and promoting staff, to spending allocations for supplies and other miscellaneous needs. It is crucial because if overspending occurs, and it continues to occur, the organization will cease to properly function and ultimately "go out of business." Therefore, properly managing budgets is vital for long-term survival and success.

What is a budget? In a nutshell, a budget is simply a guideline to keep track of spending allocation within an estimated generated income. In small, or large organizations, the finance department works closely with departmental leaders to help create such budget. However, this is an area which most new leaders have trouble understanding, especially when first promoted or hired by a new organization and seeing their budget for the first time. A spreadsheet with lots of categories and lots of numbers, and if one is lucky, someone in the finance department can help explain it.

The simplest way to understand budgeting is to compare it to a household budget or personal budget. The main consideration should be to never spend more than one makes or spend more than allocated in the current budget. A household monthly budget consists of generated income (from a job or investments), monthly bills, personal expenditures, savings, and, in some cases, retirement savings. Similarly, in the organization, their quarterly department's budget (rarely monthly) consists of allocated funds from the organization's generated revenue, expenditures, earmark funds for future projects or hires, and savings for other emergencies.

Conceptually, both types of budgets require basic mathematics, by which taking the monthly generated income, or the quarterly allocated funds, subtracting the spending, and whatever remains, will be the savings. Even though there are some complexities with organizational budgets, such as the fact it is usually on an Excel spreadsheet, and typically, the format varies from each person who created that spreadsheet. Still, the mathematical concepts of this budget are straightforward, and the spreadsheet does all the mathematical work; therefore, individuals need to learn and navigate its functions and parameters in order to fully manage it.

Forecasting

According to Investopedia.com, "Forecasting is a technique that uses historical data as inputs to make informed estimates that are predictive in determining the direction of future trends" (Tuovila 2022). In the business world, forecasting is a tool used to determine allocations for budgets and anticipate expenses for the future, and it is also used to determine the right number of staff needed for a given workday and so on.

For new and advanced leaders, this concept is necessary to learn and comprehend its usefulness during the budgeting process. It would enable each leader to manage their current tasks and plan future tasks to maintain continuous operation. In today's time, in which knowledge is at one's fingertips with many Internet tools, one can effortlessly learn the basics of forecasting in a short time. For example, here are some steps to consider during budget forecasting:

- From the past and current budget, use the allocated funds to establish a baseline amount for the overall budget expenditures.
- Determine allocated funds expectations.
- Determine expected expenses.
- Determine savings funds.
- Execute the forecast budget.

Change Management

Undoubtedly, new leaders will face a time when they have to implement change, and this will involve a process for managing change and appropriately called "Change Management." Change management is an orderly process that requires discipline, organizational skills, and, above all, good planning. This method has been used in business, but in today's time, many industries have used it to make essential changes in their organization. There are two major popular methods: John Kotter's "8-Step Change Management Model" and Kurt Lewin's "Change Management Model" (Kotter 1995; Lewin 1947). Conceptually, both methods are similar but their approaches are slightly different. Both were proven to be effective, although most will usually pick the one that suits their personal preference.

In years past, seldom would anyone in leadership think about change management. In fact, some have seen it as a task for project managers only. Well, that's simply not true. Today, everyone in leadership has to advance some change in their organization, department, or teams, or tackle new projects. Change management tactics are a great way to be timely organized from start to finish, and certainly, Kurt Lewin and John Kotter's methods are proven to be successful:

1. *Kurt Lewin's Three Stages of Change Management Model*: In the 1940s, Kurt Lewin developed his model of managing change (Lewin 1947). The process has three major steps: Unfreeze, Change, and Refreeze. The analogy that most have described this process as a square ice cube, melted down, reshaped, and refrozen into a cone. Unfreeze refers to the first stage of change, by which a leader must prepare the organization to accept change by breaking down the existing practices (assuming it's inefficient). This entails persuasive communication, from the reason change is necessary to expected outcomes. The next step is the actual changes that must occur. Lastly, Refreeze, which once the change happened, and others have accepted it, the changes are stabilized in operations.

2. *John Kotter's Eight-Step Change Management Model*: In 1995, John Kotter, a professor at Harvard School of Business, took a different approach from Kurt Lewin's model, yet developed in his work, by introducing the Eight-Step model for managing and leading change (Kotter 1995). In John Kotter's model, the eight steps are more defined, with more categories than Kurt Lewin's model, and to utilize it effectively, one has to follow every step in managing and leading change. Here are the following steps:
   - **Step 1 Establish an Urgency**: By persuading others in the organization, one must establish the need for change to an existing problem or ineffective processes. As with Kurt

Lewin's Unfreeze stage, one has to describe the reason for the change but also the end result of the change.

- **Step 2 Build a Coalition**: Depending on the project, one has to create a coalition of individuals with diverse skill sets who have vested interests in the project. These individuals will partner with the project leader to assist with planning, communicating, and executing the project.

- **Step 3 Develop a Vision**: Once an individual establishes an urgency for change, he or she should have an idea of the vision for change. With the help of the coalition, develop a vision of the intended outcome of the project, considering a few factors, such as the purpose of the project and how it will positively affect all employees. The vision should be simple yet descriptive enough to give a clear idea of the project.

- **Step 4 Communicate the Vision**: The project vision communication must have some strategic approach. For instance, determining the exact contents of the communication, the sources of communication, the timing of the communication, and whether it will be for all staff or groups of staff. Thereafter, determine whether communication is needed multiple times.

- **Step 5 Remove Obstacles**: As with any changes in the organization, there will be resistance, and it can be employees, influential leaders, or both. In this stage, the leader of the project and the coalition must anticipate such resistance and remove it by preparing a rebuttal for any negative assertions of this project. It might require internal or external expert support for this endeavor.

- **Step 6 Create Short-Term Wins**: As the project progresses, and the teams have made significant results in different stages of the project, the project leader must recognize their success and reward them in each successful stage. Not only does this tactic help maintain team motivation, but it reinforces their successful efforts.

- **Step 7 Build on the Change**: While celebrating each win is important, it is also important to maintain the momentum to finish the project and avoid complacencies during this process. One tactical method is to analyze the efforts that were successful and unsuccessful and learn from the failed efforts while building on the successful ones.

- **Step 8 Anchor the Changes in the Organization Culture**: For change to be significant, it must be embedded in the culture of the organization, which requires some strategic approach. Depending on the project, the project leader of the coalition should consistently communicate the success of the project to the staff in various means, such as staff meetings, newsletters, company websites, and other ways necessary. If the project coincides with the values of the organization, it should be included in the new hire orientation.

Both Kurt Lewin's and John Kotter's models are effective, but it depends on the individual's or the team's preferences. For some professionals, following eight steps might seem cumbersome, yet simple to follow because it fits their approach to managing the process. Other professionals might prefer the three-steps concept, which might allow them to complete the project faster, even though Kurt Lewin's model does not consider celebrating wins with the team; this step is important in today's working environment.

Management by Objectives

Management by Objectives (MBO) process has been proven to be effective, especially for new leaders in the workforce. The concept was first introduced by Peter Drucker in 1954 (Drucker 1954). The MBO is a process for defining clear objectives between management and employees, by which employees must perform to complete the objectives, and at the end of the process, management will appraise the finalized objective work.

Examples of an MBO process:

1. *Review Organizational Objectives*: Leader's overall goal is to increase employee retention by 15 percent.
2. *Set Objectives*: Leader assigns the key staff the objective task of increasing retention by 15 percent.

3. *Monitor Progress or Challenges*: Leader and key staff will meet regularly to monitor progress or evaluate challenges, in which the leader will assist to ensure the tasks are moving forward.
4. *Evaluate*: The leader evaluates the end results of the staff's efforts. The process is to ensure the objective task of increasing 15 percent retention was successful.
5. *Reward*: Assuming the objectives were met, the leader rewards the staff, which can be in a monetary form, such as a bonus, or pursue other reward and recognition matters designed by the organization.

Today, this process has become a standard in the workplace, and it has similarities to the Performance Management system, such as setting objectives for an employee, evaluating his or her performance, and rewarding. The MBO is designed for setting organizational objectives, which might include the mission, values, and strategic plan of the organization.

Time Management

As a staff professional becomes a new leader (whether it be a supervisor or a manager), there will be a noticeable change in the daily workflow. No longer this professional is bound to the normal staff's duties, rather he or she will have more daily duties to manage. This part of leadership is rarely discussed when staff are first promoted to supervisor and rarely discussed in leadership training. Unfortunately, the solution has always been to teach or encourage these new leaders to multitask, which now has been seen as a mistake by most professionals. Multitasking is the practice of completing several tasks in the same period of time, and while the idea may seem reasonable, the results of multitasking are usually projects not fully completed, or duties performed with less than 100 percent effort. However, today, successful leaders have embraced the concept and practice of Time Management.

Basically, time management is a thoughtful process. It is the process of organizing and planning how to divide one's time between specific tasks. It is designed to allow others to work efficiently on various projects or daily tasks. One keynote, there are many strategies for time management, and an individual can develop their own, but, there some simple strategies one can use as a guideline, for example:

1. Organize daily, weekly, and monthly tasks by prioritizing the important from the unimportant ones.
2. Determine which task is urgent or nonurgent, even though such tasks may all be important.
3. Create a daily, weekly, and monthly schedule for each task to be completed.
4. Maintain schedule.
5. Review the schedule daily to determine completion status of the daily, weekly, or monthly tasks.
6. Lastly, make time management part of the daily routine.

Professional Presentation

In years past, professional presentation was not only encouraged but required in order to be in any leadership role. Today, there are clear struggles among emerging leaders as to what it takes to have a professional presentation. Is it appearance, communications, conduct, or all? The short answer is yes, all the above: appearance, verbal, nonverbal, written communication, and conduct. (Written and verbal communication will be covered in more detail in Chapter 6: Human Skills.)

Appearance: There is an assertion that how one dresses is not as important as it should be, and it should not be a factor in the professional workplace. Perfect examples are some of the leaders of the High-Tech World, such as Mark Zuckerberg and the late Steve Jobs, who are consistently in t-shirts and rarely in a professional suit, yet because they are successful, it is accepted as a professional norm.

However, there are two schools of thought on this topic. One indicates that as long as leaders are successful and credible, professional attire is insignificant. While others will argue that professional attire is part of the whole platform of being professional. The argument will continue, and there might be a change in the future, but one thing we know for a fact is that there are certain times when professional attire is required, such as in court proceedings, legislative hearings, professional job interviews, and so on.

Traditionally, it has been determined that professional clothing is necessary for one's professional credibility. However, professional clothing does not necessarily mean suits for men and women. It could also be uniforms, such as those worn by Police Officers, Firefighters, Military personnel, or even service professionals like car mechanics. These uniforms represent specific professions within the structure of the organization. The public knows that when they see a police officer, they know he or she is a cop and so on. Similarly, for those leaders who work in a corporate structure (whether for profit or not), professional attire is an essential part of their presence, specifically when formally addressing staff or presenting in a public forum.

Nonverbal Communication: This is basically the expression of emotions without the use of words. Typically, it is expressed with one's facial features, such as a smile, which shows happiness or pleasure, or if it is a frown, which indicates displeasure of some type. In our society, body language and facial expression can mean various emotional manifestations, or in some cases, show no emotions. Either way, it is a part of our communications as human beings.

On most occasions, people have the tendency to attempt to read others by their body language, especially facial expressions. At times, a person can sit in deep thoughts without any facial expression, yet you will find others attempting to read this person's thoughts and likely making presumptuous conclusions. What this shows is that humans are accustomed to nonverbal communication, in spite of any verbal language. In essence, nonverbal communication is universal throughout every country and culture.

For leaders, it is important to be very conscious of one's body language and facial expression at all times. For example, having an important conversation with a staff member or a colleague with a "what the hell are you talking about" look is disrespectful, and, in most cases, is unnecessary. Sitting or standing in an awkward way might make someone feel uncomfortable. Remember, the professional environment is not intended to be as comfortable as one's home or their favorite hangout.

Professional presence is a vital part of their overall leadership credibility. All professional leaders must make nonverbal communication intentional rather than reactive. He or she must show concern, empathy, disagreement, agreement, or other when the occasion calls for it, but again, without overreacting. While some might think overreaction is a good sign of someone caring, to many others, it shows a lack of emotional control and discipline. As we are all humans, at times, overreaction will occur. Nonetheless, as professionals, being conscious and intentional of nonverbal communication will reduce overreaction. Some might not be aware that overreaction by one (verbal or nonverbal) can disrupt good communication, and it might be difficult to recover from it in a short or long time.

CHAPTER 6

Human Skills

Common scenario: Imagine, an individual has just been promoted, or hired as the new manager to lead a staff. This manager does not have any leadership experience or training. A major part of this individual's duties is to position the staff for success by managing them to their full potential. Additionally, this individual understands that the staff will follow his or her command because it is part of the organization's chain of command, in which managers lead and staff follow.

But is it that simple to command others and expect them to perform at their full potential? Are human beings easily led? Studies have shown, people will follow the command of their supervisor or manager in order to maintain their current employment with the organization, but not necessarily work at their full potential unless they are persuaded to do so (Merchant 2010; Winston 2022). As one great man once said:

> *I suppose leadership, at one time, meant muscles; but today, it means getting along with people.*
>
> —Mahatma Gandhi

Not only Gandhi was a great influential leader, but he also understood human beings, and, throughout the years, developed strong human skills, which allowed him to become a great leader.

Leaders are human beings leading other human beings, so it stands to reason that leaders must develop strong human skills, and it begins with establishing *Credibility*. Credibility is not a mere *concept* which others discuss but rather an everyday *conduct* that must be practiced daily. Yet, establishing credibility is no easy task. Credibility is truthfulness in all areas of leadership, from knowledge of the profession to ethical behavior. To establish credibility takes some steps, it starts with communication.

Basic Communications

Before you speak, listen. Before you write, think.
—William Shakespeare

There is a certain art to communication, whether it be in writings, such as with William Shakespeare, or by visual expression, as with art paintings of Michelangelo, or like Dr. Martin Luther King Jr. who was a great and powerful speaker of his time. Indeed, communication can be very powerful in various ways, though, for new leaders who enter the management world, they first need to understand communication at a basic level. Basic communication is a mutual exchange of thoughts between two or more individuals. It requires listening, talking, and, in our modern-day work, e-mail reading and writing.

Active Listening

The cliché, "You might be listening but you're not hearing." Well, this statement has some validity. Many of the communication issues arise out of employee relations, labor relations, and other conflicts in the workplace because individuals are talking to each other, yet no one is listening to any of the conversations. Certainly, we have all been there with our family arguments, in which arguments escalate to yelling because no one is listening to each other, only talking loudly at each other. Of course, being human beings, this happens in the workplace regularly at all levels, from executive to regular staff.

For leaders, a lack of listening can be very damaging to one's professional credibility, so it is an important skill that all leaders must develop. There is no exact method for learning to be an active listener, but there are some basic skills and behavior that most active listeners share:

- patient and disciplined;
- listening with intent;
- focusing on the speaker without interrupting;
- ability to identify relevant facts from the speaker;
- asking relevant questions; and
- summarizing relevant facts to the speaker.

To illustrate, let's examine a common scenario in the workplace which occurs regularly: *An employee who is very emotional comes to you with a problem that needs resolution. That employee has difficulty expressing their issue clearly, and in fact, he or she is drifting from one potential problem to another.* As an active listener, you will be able to determine the real issues and the severity of each issue. It will also allow you to write better notes in order to properly document this situation and others like them.

Verbal Communication

Great speakers throughout our time were able to utilize their preferred language to express themselves to others in a clear, concise, and persuasive manner, which most have developed through the years. Contrary to some beliefs, strong verbal communication is not something people are born with; in fact, strong verbal communication is a craft that needs to be learned and practiced, especially for leaders in any field. Again, as with Active Listening, there are no exact methods to improve verbal communication, yet there are some methods one can practice and it requires some discipline and exercise:

1. Practice verbalizing with complete sentences and proper grammar and without any jargons.
2. Practice pronouncing difficult words which will clarify communication more.
3. Use simple words as much as possible for everyone's understandings.
4. Know your audience before speaking.
5. Develop methods to control emotions, utilizing a monotonic (continuing sound with an unchanging pitch) voice. This is especially helpful during any conflict resolution, negotiations, or other matters that can raise emotions. On many occasions, if a person uses a loud voice and appears aggressive, it can be construed as a lack of confidence. This is a pitfall many leaders fall into subconsciously.
6. On the subject of voice tones, it is not *what* you say, but *how* you say it. On many occasions, managers will have a tough conversation with their staff member(s), and it might be a sensitive topic, embarrassing situation, or disciplinary proceedings. Diplomatic skills are critical in all these tough situations and also beneficial in other circumstances.

One of the most important diplomatic skills is practicing good Etiquette, such as greeting individuals, allowing others to speak without interrupting them, and simply acknowledging them.

Ability to Influence

Great communication can be gauged by how well someone connects with others and sways them with his or her message. To be influential is the highest standard of communication excellence and one of the most significant parts of being a credible leader.

Influential individuals can be any human being, regardless of whether they are in leadership roles or not. They are influential because they are credible, or some might say, they are credible because they are influential. Either way, both elements are highly important for good leadership.

Still, being influential can be a double-edged sword. One can inspire and empower others to do great things, or one can lead them on a path of destruction. History has many examples of both scenarios and also history has revealed that being influential is a powerful device. Yet, to be an influential leader, there are some basic behavior and skills one should do or in some cases not do:

1. *Making false promises*: One of the major pitfalls of leadership is making promises, which one cannot fulfill. This is one of the cases in which leaders should not do. New leaders, whether it be in politics, business, or any other had often made promises to others for improving the current situation(s). However, once those promises are not fulfilled, these leaders would appear to have failed to tell the truth, or it would appear they made frivolous promises. Either way, the credibility of these leaders is compromised, and their followers may not believe or trust them in the near future. Even though, such leaders might have worked hard to fulfill these promises, unfortunately, they faced unforeseen circumstances that prohibited them from doing so.

   a. This scenario is very common, and yet year after year, it is repeated by many leaders. The solution is very simple: leaders should never make promises that have a high risk for failure, rather leaders should make a promise to do the best they can to achieve these objectives and elaborate on the challenges of attempting to achieve it.

2. *Being transparent and consistent*: Influential leaders are often transparent and consistent with their everyday behavior and practices. They typically say what they mean, and they mean what they say. There are many benefits to it, which include the following: Clear and constant communication and messaging to employees. Staff are able to predict their leader so they are able to anticipate his or her expectations. Leaders are more likely to be equitable with their staff and are more likely to develop trust faster with staff. Lastly, being transparent and consistent shows honesty and integrity, which strengthens one's influential abilities.

3. *Building relations with others*: Leaders cannot influence others if they cannot build relationships with different people and with different positions they hold. It is a core skill that many great influential leaders have that they developed throughout the years. There are two steps to building relations with others, one, the First Contact meeting between individuals, and second, Maintaining Good Relations throughout time.

   a. **The first contact** sets the stage for communication (whether it be positive or negative) and sets the impression for the present and possible future relationship. Mainly, one has to be friendly and genuine but also thoughtful of the following:

      i. Do not make personal judgment of the person's appearance, racial profile, style, age, or any other characteristics different than one's self.

      ii. Being humble during first contact is critical, not only it shows confidence but also good manners.

      iii. Be empathetic; in other words, put yourself in the other person's place and imagine how he or she feels in their position.

      iv. Find some common ground with another because every human being has things in common; it is a matter of discovering it.

   b. **Maintaining good relations** can be very challenging for leaders; in fact, for most people. Whether it be with friends, significant others, or colleagues and staff, maintaining good relations is an ongoing important process. There is no exact method of doing so, and every leader should develop their own method. However, there is a certain fundamental behavior which helps with cultivating relationships with others, such as applying proper etiquette by conducting one's self with integrity, honesty, respect for others, and sincere care for the individual(s). As many will observe, leaders with strong influence never lose sight of sustaining relations with others; it is a major factor in being influential.

4. *Professional written communication*: Too many misunderstandings occur from unclear e-mails, texts, company ads, public statements, and more. With today's social media use (both for business and private), clear, concise, and proper writing has become challenging for many and, unfortunately, even with some leaders. A leader's ability to influence must not be limited to verbal communication, rather a leader must communicate well in writing, especially in professional environments. Still, for some new leaders, writing might be more challenging because they may not have the training of other professionals, so it is recommended to learn or evaluate basic grammar and follow professional e-mail etiquette, such as:

   a. Begin every e-mail with a friendly greeting and end with a customary "thank you, best regards" and other professional goodbyes.

   b. Do not use popular jargon in your greetings and goodbyes, such as Ciao, Cheers, and others. It lacks professionalism, and it could appear disrespectful for those who may not understand it.

   c. While drafting an e-mail or responding to an e-mail, use simple sentence structure, with proper grammar and spelling, and do not forget to read your draft before sending.

   d. Keep it as concise as possible. Every paragraph in a professional e-mail should have full substance, and anything that appears to be conversational should be eliminated.

   e. *One caveat: There will be times when conversational e-mails are acceptable with others, but one must be able to distinguish the difference between the two and not mistakenly converse in a professional e-mail.*

Resolving Conflicts

In a workplace environment, conflicts among staff and/or management occur regularly and randomly. Unfortunately, it happens for many reasons, and in some organizations, it happens more often than others. The main concern is, if a conflict escalates without resolution, it can have a long-term negative impact on both the organization and staff.

Typically, the process of conflict resolution is managed by those professionals in the human resources department, so why must managers learn to resolve conflicts? Managers work directly with their staff and have the opportunity to resolve any issue swiftly before it escalates to bigger problems. Moreover, because managers are the leaders of their staff, the staff will always look for guidance and solutions from their leader, so it is imperative for leaders to learn the basic concepts of conflict resolution. Preferably, it is best to identify potential conflict and take some action to avoid escalation. Like many problems, conflicts have symptoms, and like medical science, these symptoms are signs of irregularities.

Symptoms of potential conflict: In many situations, signs of conflicts are obvious, but on rare occasions, the signs of conflicts are subtle and can be deceiving. For leaders, they need to be observant of their staff's daily behavior, and at times, determine whether an individual staff or a group of staff member's conduct is out of their normal behavior makeup. As an example, if two people are debating or having disagreements during work, it may not be cause for alarm unless both parties stop communicating with each other for more than three days, or the debate continues in an unfriendly manner. In this situation, intervention is necessary before it escalates to a situation that is very hard to control. There are signs to look for potential conflicts, and the list can be considerable. However, if leaders notice their staff are *discontented*, *disconnected*, and *disengaged*, leaders must examine further as these are key elements of potential conflicts.

Basic steps to resolving conflicts: There are different methods to resolving conflict, and most experienced professionals have learned the basics at the beginning stage. In time, they developed their own method throughout the years, but without losing sight of the basic steps.

Here is an example of the basic conflict resolution steps:

1. Meet with each party separately and obtain all the facts which led to the dispute. However, take into account that each party might be emotional and may make random and personal statements not relevant to the actual dispute. In this situation, listening for the relevant facts and repeating those facts to the staff member(s) will help clarify the actual issue(s) that are being disputed.

2. Ask each of the disputing parties to describe their ideal resolution or outcome. This tactic will show the intent of the parties, eliminating any guessing of each party's expectations. It will also show how reasonable or unreasonable each party might be in this dispute. There are times in which each party will ask for the most, and on certain occasions, it may be unreasonable, which will lead us to the next step.

3. This step might be a little more challenging because a leader has to find common objectives among the parties in order to have a mutual understanding. One widely used tactic is to negotiate a compromise with each party separately and come to a final agreement. This may require back-and-forth discussions with all parties until an agreement is met (see next section for the *Ability to Negotiate*).

4. Note: An important element to remember is to check the organization's policies (if any) on the disputed issue(s). It's likely it will assist or guide with any resolutions.

Ability to negotiate: All leaders should learn to negotiate because it is vital for their ability to strive in their careers. There might be times when leaders will be "on the table" during union contract negotiations, or other contract negotiations, such as representing their organization with purchasing and selling materials. Negotiating skills have many benefits, which include but are not limited to the ability to use Reasoning and Compromise in all areas of management.

What is negotiation? Simply, it is communication between two or more people in order to arrive at a beneficial agreement(s). It requires patience, empathy, diplomacy, courage, emotional control, and, above all, the ability to build relations and trust with others.

For new leaders, learning to negotiate is not an effortless task one can obtain by reading materials; in fact, it takes a combination of reading, listening, and practicing in order to obtain these skills. There are online and classroom courses individuals can take that will cover the entire subject matter and provide practice sessions, which is necessary to help individuals with applying these principles to practice. In addition, there are publications by accomplished negotiators that explain the ideas and tactics of negotiations very well, and while they may not provide practice sessions, they do establish the foundational principles of negotiations. In time, one will develop their own negotiation style and strategies, which, without a doubt, will elevate their leadership skills.

Creating a Teamwork Environment

By now, the concept of teamwork is widely accepted among most, if not all organizations. Certainly, there have been many good and different approaches to teamwork through publications and trainings. What makes the teamwork environment vital to organizations? Well, if one examines the typical organization, it is made up of people with special skills and functions that contribute to the goals and mission of the organization. The challenge will always fall on organizational leaders and their team leaders to align those skills and functions to meet the goals of the organization and fulfill its mission.

For team leaders, their job is to ensure that the staff's work is being completed in a timely manner while maintaining high morale among the team. In doing so, there are some measures team leaders must learn, if not strengthen, in order to create a teamwork environment.

- Motivation and Motivation Tactics
- *Empowering Individuals*
- Developing Individuals
- Learn to Identify Talent

Motivation and Motivation Tactics: The most effective component of the human mind is the ability to be motivated for the purpose of achieving a goal. It is the one behavior that every accomplished person possesses at a certain time(s). Motivation is a desire to achieve, and one cannot achieve without it, but this behavior is not continuous, so on many occasions, it has to be fueled. Most accomplished individuals have found their own strategies to maintain motivation, yet, even they find times when it is hard to be motivated; consequently, they rely on discipline to maintain consistency.

In the work environment, team leaders must motivate themselves, and more importantly, they must motivate their staff, but before doing so, team leaders must evaluate their staff before committing to a plan. First, let us examine the usual individuals in the workforce. Typically, there are four types:

1. The self-motivated person who is driven by goal accomplishment and may only need expectations set and/or perhaps direction. Generally, this individual tends to have high aspirations to move to higher positions.
2. The middle-of-the-road person who is there, putting in his or her time at the job, and usually meets all the requirements of the job. Depending on this person's values, he or she may be satisfied with meeting job expectations and may not have other ambitions. On the other hand, this person might need the right motivation to do more than their current job requirement.
3. The person barely meets expectations but is trying very hard to do so. This individual may not require the right motivation, but rather the right training, or perhaps job duties aligned to his or her skill sets.
4. The person who has the skills, but is not meeting any expectations, or trying to do so. This situation requires a team leader to further evaluate this individual and attempt to strategize certain methods to assist this individual to perform to standards.

Motivation Theories

There are many theories as to how to motivate individuals for various challenges in life, but in the workplace, there are limits because there is only one challenge, and that is to motivate others to do their job well.

In the past, leaders used strong tactics, like the Military Drill Sergeant approach, in which they displayed extreme dissatisfaction with their employee's work by overly critiquing projects and other work-related matters. Yet, if employees exceed their boss's expectations, that boss might give some positive feedback on their work product. The theory behind this tactic is to use more negativity and harshness to bring out the best in people. In certain circumstances, it works. We have often seen human beings endure tough challenges and overcome them, and in time, surpass them. The problem with this approach is it does not work with every personality in the workforce. It only works on those who are very resilient, but even with those individuals, there might be negative long-term impacts, such as burnout, unappreciated feelings, lack of security, and more. Today, this approach is considered a pitfall and team leaders are discouraged from practicing it.

Another, more commonly used concept (past and present) is Reinforcement and Punishment. It was first introduced by the behavioral psychologist, Burrhus Skinner (Skinner 1958). It is a straightforward concept because it acknowledges the most primal basic human behavior, which is pleasure and pain. This school of psychology maintains that behavior is determined by its consequences, whether it be reinforcement or punishment. This makes it more or less likely that the behavior will occur again. For example, in the workplace, organizations use disciplinary measures to correct behavior or actions which violate their policies while rewarding those which further the organization's goals and sustain its mission.

Although awareness of these concepts is important from a historical and learning perspective, there is more to developing motivational training for employees. One important note to remember is that motivating a group and motivating an individual takes different strategies and approaches, simply because people tend to behave differently in groups than they do one-on-one.

Group Motivation

Our society has many examples of singular individuals who have the talent for motivating groups of people, from athletic and life coaches to public figures and religious leaders. What do they all have in common? They all have an ability to provide a positive outlook for the future; in other words, hope. However, the difference between those who are successful at motivating groups versus those who are unsuccessful is the capacity for being genuine.

In the work environment, it is no different. Leaders and/or team leaders must have a genuine belief in the mission and goals of the organization and must provide a positive outlook for the future of the team and/or department, but above all, team leaders must develop their own goals and subsidiary mission for their team. The purpose of having a subsidiary mission is to be more team and/or department-specific while staying within the overall guidelines of the organizational mission. Once established, team leaders must communicate the subsidiary mission and the objectives to the team. (*Note: Objectives must have reasonable timelines.*)

Establishing Team Reward(s)

Establishing rewards for a team can be a very subjective process. Each organization has its own culture and will view rewards differently. In the United States, incentives and rewards are part of the culture, and it would only stand to reason that many American organizations would adopt these values. There are those organizations that may see things differently. While many argue people need incentives to perform at a higher level, others may argue it is about work ethics, which means those with strong work ethics will perform without expectation of rewards. Still, rewards are a form of recognition, and even those with strong work ethics enjoy being recognized for their efforts.

Team leaders must consider the following before implementing team rewards:

1. The culture of the organization and whether this practice is acceptable.
2. If acceptable, consider long-term and short-term rewards. (An example of long-term rewards is for the employee to be part of a great and accomplished team that he or she can utilize to further their career. A short-term reward would be a monetary bonus or a few more vacation days and so on.)
3. Be creative with any rewards and attempt to survey the staff as to whether they would like any reward ideas.

Maintaining Motivation

Once team leaders establish motivation for the team, the challenge becomes one of maintaining this motivation throughout months. Like rewards, there are many ways of doing so, and it takes creativity. However, team leaders must be cognitive in maintaining motivation with the team. One tactic is to reinforce the goals and the mission of the team and/ or department every few months during staff meetings and encourage open conversation as to the challenges and/or successes of work projects. Another method may include a full day, designated to team building for the purpose of improving and/or exploring new ideas.

Celebrating Small Successes

As team leaders monitor their team's progress, they must never forget to celebrate the small successes that furthered the accomplishments of the objectives. Celebrating small successes is another way of giving positive feedback to the team.

One important note to consider is that in this situation, any rewards for small successes should be relatively small, perhaps a special team luncheon or gift cards and so on. The main reason is to maintain balance between the level of success and the level of celebration; in other words, each celebration should be appropriately equal to the accomplishments, and it is up to the discretion of the team leader to determine the level of success, and how to celebrate it.

Recognizing

Every human being has the need to be recognized for their achievements. It is an emotional satisfaction that builds confidence, and respect by others and motivates individuals to continue their success. In the workplace, it is highly recommended that team leaders recognize their staff in whatever means effective. (*One keynote: recognition is paramount to building a teamwork environment. It supports developing individuals with their career paths.*)

Team leaders must identify all the individuals who are making such successful impacts on the team, whether as a group and/or individually. It sounds simple enough, yet unfortunately, for many leaders, this simple concept is difficult to practice for various reasons. For some, they overanalyze and make wrong presumptions as to how to recognize employees, while others do nothing for fear of failure.

To simplify an approach, consider the following:

a. Regularly observe staff for progress.
b. Make a conscious effort to acknowledge staff.
c. Be empathetic to the staff's challenges.
d. Thank staff through various ways, such as in person, handwritten note, or any other way. Be creative.
e. Lastly, consider building an Employee Recognition Committee, mixed with leaders and staff to create recognition ideas and ways to implement them.

Staff Supporting Staff

There are many ways to gauge whether team leaders were successful in creating a teamwork environment, but one stands out more than others, and that is staff supporting other staff or team members in achieving organizational and/or departmental objectives. On some occasions, it happens organically as a result of creating a team environment, but on other occasions, it is encouraged and influenced by team leaders.

While each team leader must find his or her own style of communication and influence to assure staff members support each other, there are past methods by other team leaders that seem to have success in building team partnerships:

1. Regular staff meetings for the purpose of conceptualizing and brainstorming new ideas or improving current practices.
2. Team leader assigns a project to multiple staff members and allows the team to manage the project with clear direction from the team leader but without micromanagement.

3. Team leader encourages the project team to celebrate their success together.
4. Team leader will always recognize the project team's efforts and success.

Empowering Individuals

In recent times, we hear the term empowerment used in the workplace as a motivational tool, management style, and an embraced value, but what does it mean? Why is it an embraced value? Empowerment is simply allowing others to become stronger or more confident by giving them independence to make decisions. It is a welcomed value because it is the opposite of micromanagement.

Micromanagement is a style of management which allows managers to control their staff on all levels, without any room for staff to make any independent decisions. Those who micromanage might argue that, since they are held accountable for their staff's work, they need to make certain that things are being completed properly. However, this practice can be time-consuming and has the tendency to exhaust team leaders. In addition, this practice leaves no room for staff to learn, both from mistakes and from accomplishments.

Throughout the years, organizations have discovered micromanagement is detrimental to their organizations, from high turnovers of skilled staff to low morale, which, of course, hinders creativity and high performance. In time, most organizations embraced the idea of empowerment, and while many employees have benefited from being empowered to achieve, some, albeit a marginal group, were unaffected by it. (See my previous discussion "*Staff Supporting Staff*" on the four types of employees.) Empowering others does not come naturally. There are steps one can learn and practice, and here are a few guidelines.

It Begins With Trust: In order for staff to feel empowered, they have to believe their team leader trusts them. For team leaders, sometimes this is a difficult undertaking since they are held accountable for any mistakes of their staff. Still, it must be done because team leaders cannot empower their staff without trusting them and allowing them to make mistakes and learn from it.

Challenge Staff With Responsibilities: Team leaders should be very mindful of assigned projects. Projects should be reasonably challenging in accordance to each person's core skills but not be overwhelming by positioning someone for failure. (See later discussion about *Developing Individuals*.)

Challenge Staff Through Brainstorming: During staff meetings, team leaders should always involve the entire staff in brainstorming conversations, whether they are seasoned professionals or novices. Basically, brainstorming is a spontaneous group discussion designed to develop new ideas or find answers to challenging questions. In these circumstances, everyone has some valuable thoughts to offer. While in some circumstances, the novice staff may not participate as much as the seasoned professionals, team leaders should give them an opportunity to be heard in another time, whether in private or during staff meetings. Sometimes, great ideas come later and not at the moment, so team leaders should give others the opportunity to discuss their ideas in another time.

Set Timelines for Both Projects and Reviews: As team leaders assign projects and responsibilities, they must allocate timelines for completion, but more importantly, they must allocate time for feedback and review. This is crucial to ensure the staff is getting the support, feedback, and guidance to succeed.

Learning From Failure: No single professional has ever succeeded without many failures. It is simply being human. Team leaders need to emphasize this point to their staff as well, as team leaders must turn failure into learning moments. (See later discussion about *Developing Individuals*.)

Recognize Their Accomplishments: Team leaders must recognize their staff's accomplishments, no matter how large or small their achievement. Recognition is a form of positive reinforcement, which is a necessary tool for empowering the staff. Even though, constructive critique can also empower individuals, if it is presented honestly with the intent to help staff members to reach their objectives.

Developing Individuals: One of the most critical roles, and some might argue the most difficult, is developing staff, whether for higher and more skilled positions or different positions that require special skill sets. There are many benefits to developing staff, which include but are not limited to talent retention, good morale in the work environment, and contributing to the continuation of the organization's objective and mission. How to begin? Should every staff member be developed?

In theory, every staff member should be developed; unfortunately, not every staff member has the desire to be developed for bigger or different positions. Some staff members are happy where they are, and of course, that is acceptable. As a team leader, he or she must learn to identify (a) those who have the willingness to be developed, (b) those individuals who have the core competencies to learn different skill sets, and (c) the time commitments for training and so forth.

However, there are those individuals who are passive about professional growth but generally have the potential to be developed for more than their current position. Nevertheless, on many occasions, these individuals are overlooked by team leaders on the presumption that, since they showed little interest in development, they must be happy in their current position. While this might be the case in certain circumstances, team leaders should nonetheless attempt to identify those who have the potential for growth, not only for the benefit of the staff but for the organization's benefit.

Learn to Identify Talent: Team leaders, whether new at leadership or have been in leadership for years, all have the need for talented individuals to be part of their team, as they all understand that talented individuals bring success to the team. Yet, time after time, team leaders seem more focused on recruiting outside talent, rather than looking within their team or organization for talented individuals that could possibly meet their criteria.

On many occasions, there are individuals who have various skills, but they are in different positions throughout the organization or on the team. In such cases, team leaders should consider identifying talent within the team or the organization before recruiting outside talent. There are many benefits to this action, including, but not limited to, strengthening morale among the team and/or organization, recognizing the talent in the organization, time and cost efficient, and the internal talent have established dedication and appreciation to the team and organization. However, if team leaders cannot identify internal talents, they must utilize the recruitment process to find talented individuals that will fulfill the need of their team and organization.

To identify internal talent, team leaders should consider the following steps:

1. Have a clear understanding of additional staff needs in the near future.
2. Define the skills and behavior needed for the future position(s).
3. Team leaders should always evaluate their team's competencies in order to determine whether any team member has the necessary skills for the new position.
4. Team leaders should look for those with strong work ethics and the passion to accomplish.
5. Team leaders should collaborate with other team leaders to identify prospective talent within other teams in the organization.
6. And lastly, team leaders must provide the opportunity for those who meet their criteria and allow them to decide whether this new position will be a suitable one for them.

Development Stage: Assuming a team leader has identified a prospective talent to be developed, and now the challenge is where to start? It begins with a vision and a goal. The vision is the expected end result from the learning stage, as both the staff member and the team leader should have the same and agreed vision before starting the training.

The Goal(s): The goal(s) are usually set by the team leader, with regularly scheduled follow-up meetings to monitor progress, engage in discussion, and assist with any challenges. In addition, such progress meetings must have timelines, from when it begins to a tentative completion date. (*Important note: Team leaders must set reasonable, challenging goals which can be achieved with resilient effort but avoid setting high goals that are impossible to achieve. Create a standard for goal setting which can be applied to others in this position in order to ensure fairness and uniformity.*)

Progress Meeting: Progress meetings must have a timeline, from the first stage of development to the last stage of accomplishment. Assuming the team leader and his or her staff have set a reasonable goal for development, thereafter, the team leader will be responsible for creating or obtaining the teaching method for development, which will include the subject matter curriculum.

The subjects in the curriculum can be used to assist with creating the progress meeting agenda. For example, the first topic on the curriculum that the staff member completes should be one of the topics to discuss in the first meeting. In these situations, the team leader must reinforce, help explain, and, on some occasions, teach. However, if the subject matter is very technical and is not within the expertise of the team leader, then the staff member should be able to explain what he or she has learned. Not only it is a good reinforcement method, but by explaining it thoroughly, it shows that the staff learned the materials well. As one would say, if they can explain it, then they have learned it.

Challenging and Teaching Moments: There is no doubt there will be challenges, failures, and at times, things do not go smoothly. This is a crucial time for team leaders to engage the staff members during this process and turn every mistake, challenge, or failure into teaching moments. Teaching moments are simply those times when you look at failures and mistakes and learn something from them, whether to evaluate and/or change the initial approach or to avoid repeating an action. Either way, this is truly the most educational period of any stage of development.

Expectation: As previously mentioned in *The Goal(s)*, both team leader and staff must have reasonable expectations of the outcome of the development. The emphasis is "reasonable," simply because there are times, when both parties may not be 100 percent satisfied with the outcome of the development, yet to avoid negative feelings and reactions, both parties must look at the positive outcomes, and learn from the negative ones. On most occasions, the development phase is positive for all parties, and as it should be. The staff member will gain knowledge and further his or her career objectives, while the team leader gains personal and professional fulfillment. Of course, the organization will benefit the most, as they would increase their staff's talent and further the mission and objectives of the organization.

Conclusion: Good relations between leaders and their followers require constant work to maintain, and it is the responsibility of the leader to monitor and make necessary adjustments when needed. There will be times when leaders will be unsuccessful in maintaining good relations with one or more staff members but learning the fundamentals of human skills will give leaders a better chance to prevent negative issues which can result in controversies. Furthermore, human skills development and improvement is an ongoing process, even if individuals are seasoned leaders. As many of them will admit, the most difficult part of their job is managing people, merely because human behavior is not a mathematical calculation. It does not follow an exact logical pattern, so it cannot easily be predicted. Rather, human behavior patterns have a probability factor, in which certain behaviors can be triggered by human actions, such as positive feedback that triggers happiness and negative feedback that triggers unhappiness.

CHAPTER 7

Ethical Conduct and Practices

It is rare to find the subject of ethics in leadership training today. In fact, like technical skills, most professional leadership trainers presume that organizations have addressed or have trained on these topics at some point in the tenure of any leader. Yet, the most critical component of a leader's credibility is her or his ethical conduct and practices, as many will discover, when leaders manage with strong principles, their staff will have high regard and faithfulness for their leaders. So, what defines ethics? Why is it necessary to include ethics in professional development? In what areas are ethics practical and relevant?

Generally speaking, ethics can be defined as a set of moral principles that describes good and bad behavior as it applies to society as a whole. The last few decades have given rise to scandals, corruption, and mistreatment of others, and the need to implement and enforce ethical conduct in the workplace has become imperative.

However, much of the ethical enforcement has been in the form of staff disciplinary actions, such as termination, suspension, or other. With such actions, many have criticized the process as being inconsistent and unfair, merely because some leaders have enforced ethical violations with their staff, yet fail to follow or hold themselves accountable for their ethical violations. Ultimately, these leaders will lose their professional credibility and no longer will they be able to lead efficiently, or develop staff commitments, especially during critical times when leaders rely heavily on staff's performances.

Applied Ethics

As new or upcoming leaders, adopting ethical principles should not be a choice, but rather a conscious everyday effort. In almost everything leaders execute, there will be right and wrong actions, inactions, and/ or decisions. By applying ethical principles into daily processes, it will strengthen the leader's ability to lead, while reducing the risk of losing trustworthiness with staff, and it begins with some fundamentals.

Performance Appraisals or Reviews

One can argue that the most controversial process is Performance Appraisals or Performance Reviews. It is controversial because it is one of the most debated processes in business as to whether it is necessary to have or not. Other issues arising from performance reviews include the dissatisfaction of employees, even when individuals receive a positive review. However, from an ethical standpoint, many employees, including management staff, have been the subject of bias and wrongful performance review outcomes, in which their direct supervisor has unjustifiably given a bad performance evaluation, made inappropriate comments in this process, and/or set unreasonable performance expectations knowing the employee cannot achieve it. Typically, the motivation behind this might be to demote from one's current position, hold back promotions, or terminate such employees for whatever personal reason(s) of that supervisor.

Like many unethical conducts, the ramifications are predictable in most cases. In the worst-case scenario, legal action would occur against the organization, and depending on the jurisdiction, the leader might be liable if he or she is proven to have intentionally harmed the employee. Other damage results may occur, such as loss of leadership credibility, team morale damage, and, of course, employee turnover, which tends to be costly for any organization and so on.

The key to addressing ethical responsibilities in the performance appraisals section is to focus on the actual evaluations of the employee's job performance for the past year or, in some cases, mid-year. It is the responsibility of leaders to be "fair and just" by evaluating each staff member in accordance to their job requirements and performance expectations, without considering any personal prejudice toward the staff member. One way of knowing that a leader has given a fair employee evaluation is by the foreseeable outcome of the performance appraisal process by both leader and staff member. If a leader has been properly communicating with his or her staff members regarding their job performance throughout the year, there should be no surprises during the performance appraisal process.

Disciplinary Actions

Similar to performance appraisals, when disciplinary action is performed improperly and unfairly, the results usually will lead to wrongful termination cases, whether in an arbitration hearing, labor commission complaint, or a jury trial. Either way, it is very costly for everyone, the plaintiff and the defendant. In essence, disciplinary actions are documenting bad performance and/or behavior by formal written warnings, correction action plans, such as a Performance Improvement Plan (PIP), and/or termination of employment. Disciplinary actions can also include suspensions and position demotions.

For every case that warrants an employee disciplinary action, leaders must consider the ethical implications before pursuing such actions, as to whether actions are necessary, fair, or if there are alternatives to disciplinary procedures. To do so, leaders must assess the facts of each possible organizational policy violation by the employee. If the facts are conclusive (as to the employee having violated policy(s)), then it would warrant disciplinary measures. However, ethical implication arises when disciplinary measures are applied discriminatory, in which one employee receives different corrective actions than others. This type of practice is unfair and can lead to legal challenges for the organization and/or the leader.

There are many other circumstances in which disciplinary measures are applied unethically, such as when leaders have a personal dislike for an employee. They make a conscious effort to attempt to find any wrongdoings by him or her to terminate this employee. Unfortunately, this situation occurs in many organizations, and it is one of the reasons for the existence of bad leadership in the workforce. For this reason, leaders must always apply ethical standards during disciplinary procedures.

Favoritism-Free Workplace Environment

Favoritism in the workforce is not a new practice; in fact, it exists among many teams throughout different organizations. Yet, while most organizations discourage this type of behavior through their workforce policies, they are rarely ever enforced, simply because, it is difficult to determine that favoritism exists without some physical evidence, such as unjustified pay promotions, pay increases, unauthorized gifts, and so on.

What is favoritism? What are the impacts of favoritism? In the workplace environment, favoritism is an act of treating one or a group better than others based on personal preference rather than professional judgment. Examples of such acts include but are not limited to:

- Promoting or hiring unqualified individuals.
- Giving unjustifiably preferable treatment to an individual and/or group while excluding others.
- Giving larger percentage salary increases for some without proper cause.
- And creating opportunities for particular individual(s) while excluding others, and so on.

As the saying goes, for every action, there is a reaction. Leaders who practice favoritism, they will eventually create an imbalanced team, department, and even organization. While the favored few are content and happy, the unfavored majority are unhappy, discontented, and disconnected in various ways. When staff are unhappy, their productivity, creative thoughts, and willingness to assist diminish. Ultimately, retaining good staff becomes difficult, and leadership credibility is compromised, and once that occurs, it becomes difficult to manage staff.

Credibility loss has its own consequences, such as damage to professional reputation that can have long-term disadvantages for future growth in the organization, or being selected for higher positions in other organizations. Moreover, if a CEO/president of any organization favors others, it becomes part of the organization's culture, which, of course, will have a larger negative impact on the organization and staff. Therefore, it is clear that there are adverse effects due to favoritism, and for leaders, favoritism should not be a choice to practice, but rather a conscious effort to avoid doing it.

Development and Promotions

Great leaders in the workplace have always been those who care about their staff, not just for health and well-being but for the development of their lives, both personally and especially professionally. This leadership principle is guided by the belief that human beings are significant, and it is the duty of leaders to improve today's challenges while setting the foundation for the next generation.

The key to developing others is to recognize their skills, core competencies, and, above all, their motivation to achieve. Yet, again, one must be mindful to avoid any personal feelings and favoritism toward certain staff members. The development and promotion stages are critical, and on some occasions, it can be controversial. It is controversial because even if the leader rightfully and justifiably promoted one or more staff members, some might claim that they were overlooked and did not get the opportunity to be developed. Unfortunately, this is a common theme among many organizations, and what some organizations have done is create proper processes for development and promotion for employees to ensure it is being practiced properly.

Certainly, there is still room for personal judgments, and this is where ethical behavior and practice must be applied, even if such leaders follow the development and promotion processes perfectly.

Creating an Open and Honest Environment

At some point in one's career, he or she will hear statements such as "great place to work, nurturing work environment, or creative atmosphere." On the opposite side, one might also hear statements such as "toxic work environment, horrible place to work, and/or oppressive workplace."

Obviously, all organizations would prefer to be called a great place to work, and so on. However, the task of doing so requires more than one action plan. It requires several plans working concurrently or, in other cases, gradually. Therefore, whether one is currently in a toxic work environment or a nurturing one, ethically speaking, as a leader, one must take steps to change and improve the bad work environment or continue to improve the great workplace.

Why should creating an open and honest work environment partly fall within the ethics training? Many employees who choose to become leaders are unaware of the higher ethical standards that come with leadership. Most understand the higher responsibilities but seldom are conscious of the ethical standards. If one begins by creating a great working environment with ethical intentions and actions, it will produce excellent results. It begins with the internal departmental or team communications.

Communication must be open and honest. This means that each staff member should be able to express their opinion and be allowed to give candid feedback regardless of whether it challenges the goals of the department or organization. For example, assuming there is an organizational initiative to make a large change, and there are prospective negative impacts that might result from this initiative, the staff must be encouraged to communicate their thoughts and concerns. Not only will this ensure that such initiative is being deliberately examined, but it is also developing open communication.

Another means of creating an open and honest environment is the ability to give and receive honest feedback, no matter how difficult the subject matter is. Of course, the contrary situation is a closed communication environment, by which leaders put forth plans and expect their staff to follow it without receiving their feedback on projects. This will likely have numerous negative impacts as a result of a closed communication team environment.

There are other action plans for creating a great working environment, and as mentioned previously, it can be implemented concurrently or gradually, but most importantly, it has to begin with ethical purpose and actions in order to be successful.

Accountabilities

One of the main duties of leadership is holding their staff accountable for job performance and/or professional behavior/conduct. That means staff must follow the appropriate laws, workforce policies and procedures of the organization, and perform their job in accordance with their job description. Failure to do so will most likely result in disciplinary actions which can lead to job termination. However, with the duty to hold staff accountable, leaders must be conscious of their personal responsibilities as leaders. By accepting a leadership role, one has accepted a position that is accompanied by higher standards in ethical conduct, job performance, and compliance with laws, policies, and procedures.

In one of his addresses to the nation, John F. Kennedy said the following:

> This Administration intends to be candid about its errors; for a wise man once said; An error does not become a mistake until you refuse to correct it. We intend to accept full responsibilities for our errors; and we expect you to point them out when we miss them. (Kennedy 1961)

Clearly, President Kennedy's intent was to be honest about any mistakes that might and would occur during his administration, but the overall message was that his administration would hold themselves accountable for any mistakes.

What does it mean to be accountable? In essence, being accountable is taking responsibility for one's actions when plans fail. For some, they refuse to be accountable for mistakes, no matter how small or large it is, simply because the results can be damaging. For instance, a person can be demoted, or terminated from their current job, or harm to their current professional reputation. Unfortunately, these types of individuals rely on a different tactic, and that is blaming others for their mistakes and/or making unjustifiable excuses rather than taking the honest path. Clearly, from an ethical standpoint, the candid approach is the right approach, and while it is tougher and can be more exhausting approach, the results are more favorable in both short and long term, especially to one's professional reputation.

Hypothetically speaking, assume President Kennedy was aware of numerous mistakes his administration had made, and rather than be candid with the public, he took the dishonest approach and tried hiding the truth. As with many lies, they are eventually discovered, and once it's discovered, the end result would be public distrust and loss of leadership credibility. Thereafter, any initiative that President Kennedy put forth would face harsh criticism from the public and other lawmakers, even if the initiative was an excellent plan. Since the president lost public trust and credibility, any attempt to gain it back would be very challenging and the probabilities are unlikely. Yet, if the president took the honest approach and acknowledged his administration's mistakes and made plans to correct such mistakes (even if it was very difficult), he would have gained more respect and certainly more trust from the public. The challenge of correcting mistakes would be far simpler than the challenge of attempting to regain trust and credibility.

Concluding the First Stage

Leadership has to have a beginning, and as new leaders enter the first stage of their leadership journey, applying the Four Fundamental Approach (FFA) principles will guide them to the next phase of leadership development. As time passes, leaders will discover that great leadership is an evolutionary process, comprising failures, mistakes, learning moments, but above all, success and fulfillment.

The Second Stage—
Emotional Development
for Leadership

CHAPTER 8

The Emotional Development for Leadership

In this stage of leadership development, individuals must prepare themselves for the daily challenges of being a leader, as many have discovered, leadership can be emotionally demanding and exhausting. While leaders hold positions of authority, and it certainly has its benefits, it does have significant drawbacks as well.

Individuals seeking leadership roles must recognize that the responsibilities of leadership outweigh its benefits. Good leaders are held at a higher standard, which means they are expected to lead with a rational approach, be the voice of reason, take responsibility for their team's mistakes, hold themselves accountable, guide others, set standards of excellence for themselves and their team, create a teamwork atmosphere, build strong relations, motivate others, resolve conflicts, and so on.

For this reason, individuals must prepare themselves emotionally as well as knowledgeably (as we discussed in the Technical Skills) in order to become good leaders. Like other developments, emotional development is a process that most human beings are capable of doing themselves, as evidenced by the end results of the Emotional Intelligence practice. In the last few decades, this concept became highly utilized by individuals in their personal and professional lives, and it continues to be used today, especially in leadership development.

Emotional Intelligence

Abraham Maslow introduced the concept of Emotional Strength in 1950, which Michael Beldoch later changed to Emotional Intelligence (Beldoch 1964; Maslow 1950). But it was in the 1990s that the Emotional Intelligence theory gained popularity through an article by psychologists Peter

Salovey and John Mayer (Salovey and Mayer 1990). Subsequently, in 1996, Daniel Goleman, a psychologist by trade and science writer for *The New York Times*, specializing in brain and behavior research, continued this theory with a different perspective in his book (Goleman 1996).

Emotional intelligence is the ability to recognize and manage emotions in an effort to build good relations with others. According to Peter Salovey and John Mayer, their concept has four components:

1. The ability to perceive emotions in oneself and others accurately.
2. The ability to use emotions to facilitate thinking.
3. The ability to understand emotions, emotional language, and the signals conveyed by emotions.
4. The ability to manage emotions so as to attain specific goals.

Similarly, Daniel Goleman's Emotional Intelligence theory has five components, yet equally relevant to the thought process of emotional intelligence:

1. Motivation
2. Self-awareness
3. Self-regulation
4. Empathy
5. Social skills

These components offer individuals a set of guidelines for emotional self-developments, but unlike traditional coaching by a licensed behavior health practitioner, individuals must first develop the self-motivation to engage and improve their discipline mindset.

Motivation

Achieving objectives requires two elements, the motivation to begin the process and the discipline to manage and finalize it. Motivation is the personal desire or drive to commit to achieving a goal(s). It is a vision of the end result of a goal, and for different individuals, it can mean anything, from completing an educational degree to being fit and so on. Yet, there are times in which all humans have difficulties being motivated, and while there are many strategies to assist with developing self-motivation, there is one tactic that is distinctive from others, and that is being decisive. To highlight the obvious, a firm-thinking mind is an effective mind; essentially, it is those individuals who can make a definite decision and, ultimately, act on it with a disciplinary mindset.

The Mindset of Discipline

The mindset of discipline refers to a state of mind in which an individual is consistently focused on the tasks or the situations at hand. It is a thought process that drives behavior to act, or in different cases, not act. All adult human beings have the ability to be disciplined, it is a learned trait necessary for survival, yet with certain degrees of focus. Those who are most accomplished have a high degree of discipline, while those who are least accomplished have a low degree of discipline.

As a leader, the degree of discipline should not be a choice, rather a daily practice. Leaders must have a high degree of discipline for many reasons, with the most important as setting an example for their staff. Improving one's disciplined mindset can be achieved with some basic fundamental steps, and it begins with deciding on a reasonable objective(s), thereafter, defining the criteria and the steps necessary to achieve such objective(s), and lastly, creating a new daily routine and diligently following it.

Self-Awareness and Perception of Others

Self-awareness is the ability to recognize, understand, and monitor emotions and their effects on an individual's performance. The ability to read personal feelings and reasons for those feelings can determine whether it will help or hinder one's actions. Self-awareness can also measure one's strengths and weaknesses, which allows proper decision making in certain circumstances. In addition, perceiving one's personal emotions permits the ability to recognize and understand the emotions of others.

This concept is rarely practiced by many leaders, partly because they are unaware of it, or if they are aware of it, they may not see the value of this concept as it relates to leadership. Yet, imagine a leader who cannot understand or recognize his or her emotions, or the emotions of others while managing and communicating with staff. The likelihood of this scenario would be a task-driven leader who is only interested in task completion by his or her staff, regardless of whether the staff is overstressed and pushed to the edge.

For leaders to be self-aware of their emotions, they must first understand basic human emotions, but more importantly, they need to recognize relevant human emotions in the workplace, such as happiness, anger, frustration, satisfaction, sadness, anticipation, panic, discontented, disrespectful, vanity, selfishness, pride, trust, surprise, and disgust. It is those emotions that, on most occasions, are triggered by the leader's behavior and actions. Fundamentally, it is a cause and an effect principle, by which a behavior that is combined with actions will likely cause certain feeling(s). For example, if a leader praises his or her staff for their work, the likelihood of the leader's action will produce happiness and satisfaction. On the other hand, if this leader belittles his or her staff, the probability of the leader's action will cause unhappiness and dissatisfaction.

The key to self-awareness is intentional consciousness of one's own emotions and behavior. It is a self-analysis routine that begins in the morning all the way to the end of the day, analyzing every action and behavior during each period of the day in order to fully understand the reasons for one's actions and behavior in various times and circumstances. To put it simply, it is a daily exercise for evaluating an individual's own behavior that in time will become a mindset routine for self-awareness.

As leaders become more self-aware of their own behaviors and actions, their ability to perceive the behavior of others becomes intuitive. Through their daily interactions, leaders will experience different emotions and conduct from staff, colleagues, and/or higher leadership. Intuitive leaders will be capable of recognizing these behaviors and decide the best course of action to take, or not to take. As William Shakespeare said "before you speak, listen. Before you write, think." While this seems to be a common-sense approach, for many, especially those in leadership roles, it has not been the case. Too many ineffective leaders tend to react before analyzing the situation(s), jump to a conclusion without fully understanding the facts, and respond with a lack of intelligence. Yet, for those leaders with strong behavior perceptions, they will undoubtedly avoid any of these pitfalls of overactions.

Self-Regulations or the Ability to Manage Emotions

As leaders become more self-aware of their own behavior and actions, it becomes critical to manage these behaviors in order to become better leaders. Controlling one's emotions is likely one of the most difficult mental training that leaders must do, in that at some point in every leader's career, he or she will be challenged, pushed, and tested in various situations that require emotional control. The importance of emotional control has numerous benefits for leaders, especially during extreme and stressful situations. It allows leaders to maintain a rational mind, avoid panic, and make proper decisions. In addition, controlling one's emotions maintains the ability to reason and avoid a clouded mind, which is a mind filled with anxiety, apprehension, fear, doubt, and overall insecurities.

However, we are human beings and we are inherently emotional with various degrees of behavior expressions, and while being fully in control of one's emotions may not be realistic, managing key emotions during certain situations is more likely achievable and highly desirable. For example, these key emotions are as follows.

Anger

For many, this is considered one of the most unattractive emotions that a human being possesses. So much so, that there are courses on anger management practically everywhere, given the fact that when anger is not managed properly, it has detrimental consequences. Though, anger is also considered a defense mechanism to threatening situations, and in some circumstances, it is necessary for self-preservation. However, in leadership, anger should only be a choice under extraordinary situation(s), but in most cases, anger must be controlled without any display. (*Case in point: Several leaders and staff were in a meeting discussing opposing issues, and one leader became angry and displayed it by raising her or his voice while shouting directly at others in the room. Thereafter, the entire room became silent, while the conversation about the issues ceased to continue, and nothing was resolved that day.*) This behavior is unacceptable and nonproductive, and it clearly demonstrates a lack of emotional intelligence to everyone, which ultimately causes credibility damage.

Vanity

There is level of pride in one's accomplishment(s), which is considered healthy for an individual's self-esteem. Then, there is a level of pride that is believed to be excessive enough to be called vain. Vanity encompasses many unfavorable behaviors, such as arrogance, stubbornness, disrespectful attitude, close-mindedness, and general impoliteness. These behaviors can be seen by many bad leaders in various leadership roles, whether it be in business, government, nonprofits, and so on. (*Case in point: In one situation, a leader was facing a tough decision that required careful thinking from all sides of the issue(s). Unfortunately, this leader made a final decision without considering all the possible factors of the issue(s), or without considering other professional opinions, and refused to listen to his or her support staff. The impact of this leader's decision was detrimentally foreseeable.*) This leader's behavior is a classic example of a person who does not value the opinions of others and thinks that he or she knows best. Many have seen this behavior in their workplace and unfortunately, it still exists in many organizations.

Vindictiveness

In the professional world, there have always been disagreements, conflicts, and misunderstandings. It is, of course, part of being a human being. Yet, in those situations, it is always important that there are resolutions without consequences. Many leaders have been involved in situations in which others have disagreed or complained against them and found themselves in a situation that would allow them to be vindictive. For good leaders, vindictive conduct is not within the scope of their behavior because it has damaging effects from the legal, ethical, and leadership credibility factors. (*Case in point: A whistleblower employee reported her or his manager for an alleged policy and legal violations. The investigation took months to complete and found no liability for the manager's conduct. This manager was stressed for a long time and upset about the individual who she or he believes was wrongfully and recklessly accused.*) Whistleblowers are protected by law from any retaliations, which is usually supported by company policies in most organizations. Yet, in this scenario, one can understand the manager's temptation to retaliate against this whistleblower employee; however, doing so will likely result in legal actions, company policy violations, loss of leadership credibility, and overall professional reputation damage. Therefore, it is imperative in such situations that leaders manage their emotions and thoughtfully consider every action step.

Dismissive

Bad leaders have the tendency to dismiss the opinions, feelings, accomplishments, and credentials of others. Rarely discussed in leadership topics, yet often practiced by bad leaders. It is a disrespectful behavior that is often noticed from the first or second interactions with a bad leader. (*Case in point: During a staff meeting, the new manager presented plans for the future of the department. Unfortunately, this manager designed the plans without discussing the relevant challenges currently existing with staff and/or other management team. Once the presentation was completed, staff members asked whether they can ask questions and give some helpful feedback, the manager reluctantly agreed, but staff would have to e-mail their questions and comments. Thereafter, several staff members responded by giving very helpful suggestions, only to be ignored by the manager.*) While this is a hypothetical situation, it is regrettably common in the workplace, and it is typical behavior from a leader that lacks emotional intelligence.

Empathy

The ability to comprehend the feelings of others is essentially the description of empathy. This concept has been discussed in the workforce (especially in leadership topics) for some time now, mainly because of the undesirable work environment that was created by certain leaders who lacked empathetic conduct. It is the type of environment in which people are judged harshly for mistakes, perceived mistakes, or other matters, such as personal preferences and personality types.

On the other hand, there are those leaders who consistently empathize with their staff's feelings and the emotions they are experiencing during certain times because, at some point in their career, these leaders have experienced the same situation(s) and understand what their staff are feeling. (*Case in point: During a project, a leader assigned a staff member a challenging task, even though this staff member had never done this task before. The leader had confidence that this staff member would complete the task in time because this individual had the right competency for the task. However, with the pressure of completing this project on time coupled with errors, the staff member failed to complete it in a timely manner. The leader was not upset and accepted accountability for his or her staff. When the leader was asked as to why he was not upset, the leader replied by saying, "in the beginning of my career, I faced similar challenges, and the situation was overwhelming, and I too have failed at the task."*) Regardless of whether this leader had a similar experience during his youthful career, it was his or her ability to be human and understand the feelings of others during certain circumstances. Rather than seeing failure, this leader perceived this incomplete task as a learning experience. Empathy is a behavior that can transfer from one human being to another throughout time, but it takes one person to start this behavior practice and it will soon be continued by other individuals. As with this hypothetical case, because this leader was able to be empathetic with his or her staff member, there is a strong likelihood that if this individual becomes a leader, he or she will continue this learned behavior of empathy with his or her staff.

The Ability to Use Emotions to Facilitate Thinking

One of the main components in the Peter Salovey and John Mayer emotional intelligence model is the ability to use emotions to facilitate thinking in various situations (Salovey and Mayer 1990). The simplest example is a coach who can recognize an area of his or her team's development and utilize emotions to generate motivational behavior that will support certain team objectives.

In the last few decades to the current times, this area of emotional intelligence has been the focus of most (if not all) leadership training throughout the United States, for the reason that it is an effective method of motivating staff. Yet, developing this area of emotional intelligence requires the emotional awareness of others (as described previously), and the ability to identify each staff's personality traits. (*Case in point: A seasoned leader had accepted a new position for an organization with a dysfunctional department. The department was dysfunctional because of the previous leader who had led by authority and failed at empowering staff and building confidence within the team. The new leader took a different approach and decided to meet each individual staff member in order to understand each of their personality, motivation, professional strength, area of development, personal likes and dislikes. In doing so, the leader discovered various differences as well as commonalities among the staff. This allowed the leader to properly utilize different behavior methods to motivate, empower, and build confidence in the team.*)

Unfortunately, with bad leaders governing many areas of the workforce, they have used behavior tactics that generated negative staff emotions such as fear, panic, hatred, anger, division among teams, and so on. This action has resulted in high employee turnovers, poor productivity, and created an unpleasant work environment. Eventually, and on most occasions, these leaders either will face litigation, be pushed out of the organization, or both. Therefore, as leaders evolve, they must learn and practice this key component of emotional intelligence as it is intended.

Social Skills

If emotional intelligence is designed to improve human interactions, then it is no surprise that social skills are included as one of the categories of emotional intelligence by Daniel Goleman (Goleman 1996). Broadly speaking, social skills combine key behaviors that allow human beings to positively interact with one another. But to paraphrase Daniel Goleman, social skills are the emotional intelligence skills to appropriately manage one's and other's emotions, to connect, interact, and work with others (Goleman 1996). Of course, there are other acceptable definitions that define social skills as: "Any competence facilitating interaction and communication with others where social rules and relations are created, communicated, and changed in verbal and nonverbal ways" (Emeri 2022; Rani and Dhanda 2018).

No matter how social skills are defined, the main theme is the same: proper human interaction through appropriate behaviors. While this sounds simple, there are many factors to consider that contribute to social skills norms, such as racial customs, local culture, specific business culture, and overall, the country's values that drive the culture and define its social skills. These factors can determine certain acceptable behaviors, and at the same time, it can be challenging when applying one culture's behavior to a different cultural setting.

(*Case in point: In many traditional cultures (that might be described as countries with long ancient history), proper etiquette is highly valued and expected; from appropriate greetings to dressing suitable for the exact occasions and so forth. It is in fact the social norm for those who have been raised in this environment, which of course defines their social skills. Yet, in the workforce today, where diversity and inclusion are inevitable, there are many individuals with different types of upbringings with various social norms that comprise assorted social skills. These diverse social skills can have an adverse effect on one another if one dominates the others with the expectations for the others to conform.*) Fortunately, in today's time, the majority of organizations have become aware and sensitive to people with diverse backgrounds and adopted policies and practices which affect their company culture by ensuring a certain social norm balance between everyone.

This social norm balance helps create social skills that everyone can adapt to, with the intent of maintaining a healthy professional relationship among everyone. Fundamentally, it is the social skills that all the world cultures have in common, such as friendliness, courtesy, hospitality, respect, and overall civilized behavior through proper manners. It is also, being disciplined and thoughtful during conversations, understanding conversational topic boundaries, and eliminating being intrusive and presumptuous.

Social skills are a critical component of emotional intelligence, but more importantly, it is a critical element in leadership. Imagine a leader who does not have social skills; this person would simply be considered a boss who only commands his or her staff without adequate human interactions.

Third Stage Conclusion

As leaders become stronger at managing their own emotions, soon after, these leaders will discover that it becomes easier to positively lead others in various settings. Having or developing emotional intelligence should not be a choice but rather a requirement for another method for advancing one's leadership skills.

The Third Stage—
Advanced Leadership Skills

CHAPTER 9

Advanced Leadership Skills

One might think that advanced leadership skills are for those at the higher-level positions, such as for Chief Executive Officers (CEO) and other executive-level positions. Well, this is not true, simply because these advanced skills can apply to most leadership roles in the organization (Moldoveanu and Narayandas 2019). However, such advanced skills are not developed in a short period of time, rather it is part of the evaluation of good leadership. Indeed, great leadership is an evolutionary process, which combines leadership training development with years of practical application.

The Vision

A visionary leader is a leader who is above and beyond other leaders. It is one of the elements that sets the average leader apart from one who is above average. Generally speaking, visionary leaders in the business world tend to be CEOs, which stands to reason since they must have a vision for the overall success of the organization, from financial stabilities to a great working culture. Yet, to create a vision, it must be accompanied with a workable and achievable plan of action. While many leaders had extraordinary visions, they failed during the implementation stages because they lacked the workability elements. Or in another case, the vision was achieved by overly pushing employees to the brink of high levels of stress, which ultimately resulted in high turnovers of top talent.

In the beginning stages of developing a vision for the success of the organization, leaders must evaluate and assure that all aspects of the organization are working efficiently, but more importantly, leaders must evaluate their internal talent to determine whether they can assist with furthering the vision. On many occasions, such internal talent may not exactly meet the requirements of the new leader, which ultimately creates the first challenge with implementing his or her vision. However, experienced good leaders understand that this scenario is more likely in organizations today than the contrary. These leaders also recognize that they must utilize the strength of their current talent rather than focus on their areas of difficulties.

CEOs must ultimately create and set the vision for the entire organization, while other leaders in the organization must create their vision for their department, and it must tie into the CEOs' organizational objectives. On many occasions, it is more challenging based upon the following reasons: (1) Typically, it is not expected for leaders other than CEOs to have a vision. (2) To customize their vision to the CEO's objective while creating their own vision for their department requires a certain level of creativity. (3) These departmental leaders must be able to persuade their staff as well as the CEO of their departmental vision. One example of a departmental leader's vision is to create an efficient department, from administering processes fulfilling the organization's needs to creating a collaborative environment.

Ultimately, a visionary leader is a leader who has entered the advanced stages of leadership, and while it is one of the elements of mastering leadership, it is, nonetheless, one of the most important.

Building Relations

There are certain expectations advanced leaders must perform, even though it is rarely expressed in leadership training, and at times, it is only implied in job descriptions. One of those critical expectations is that advanced leaders must be able to pursue, build, and maintain professional relations with others, which includes staff, colleagues, networks, and various other professionals. The value of relations with others is unlimited, from building business network and learning from others, to establishing leadership in the community.

Many successful advanced leaders recognize that some of their organizational success was due to the relationships they created with others. It was those relationships that helped drive their objectives in various ways. For example, beginning with the relationship one CEO had with another CEO, he or she managed to create a merger of two organizations.

Unfortunately, some of the newer leaders cannot see the significance of this practice simply because it is difficult to measure its success, and it requires additional work. Moreover, many of these newer leaders tend to focus on what they believe is the most tangible path to success, which is usually within the comfort zone of their trained profession. Regrettably, these types of leaders will ultimately limit their own abilities to mature as seasoned, advanced leaders and will eventually fall into mediocrity, as with many in the last few decades.

Successful advanced leaders begin building relations in various ways. In the professional world, they become Board Members to different organizations, from mission-driven nonprofits to businesses of their own interests. There are benefits to become a board member:

1. Expanding network.
2. Learn and discover how other businesses operate.
3. Expand company and personal brand.
4. Make a difference by incorporating one's expertise to help the organization.
5. Strengthening leadership credibility.

Another common method that successful advanced leaders have utilized to build relations is through Community Involvement and Government Relations. With community involvement, leaders will have the opportunity to give back and help those in the community who are in need. Many leaders have shared their experience with their community involvement and found that it gave them different perspectives on life, and in many ways, it strengthens their leadership, specifically with their human skills.

On the other hand, with Government Relations, the main focus for leadership involvement is to develop relations with public officials that can limit or advance the functions of the organization during the legislation process. For example, some profit-driven organizations with great missions, such as in the industry of solar and renewable energies, highly depend on their lobbyist to advocate for legislation that is friendly to the industry. However, these lobbyists cannot succeed without the assistance of organizational leaders, for the main reason that these lobbyists must understand the existing issues that obstruct the industry from moving forward. On many occasions, there are organizational leaders that have developed and maintained relations with public officials without the assistance of their lobbyists and were able to influence public officials on legislation that helped further their industry interests.

Clearly, building and maintaining relationships is valuable for organizations, and in the last few years, the board of directors of various industries began expressly setting expectations for organizational leaders to develop, maintain, and strengthen relationships, especially with communities and government officials.

Influential

Arguably, one of the most important components of leadership is the ability to influence others. History has shown us many examples of great influential leaders, such as Dr. Martin Luther King Jr., Mahatma Gandhi, Abraham Lincoln, Mother Teresa, and others. One can easily say that the strength of a leader can be measured by the impact that the leader had created through his or her ability to be influential. Yet, there are still leaders today (even in advanced stages) who believe that being influential is being in a position of power and utilizing it by commanding and coercing others to achieve. Unfortunately, this mistaken belief that influence is best performed by positions of power is as prevalent today as it was in the past.

Influential leaders are those who, through their influential proficiencies, achieve results through individuals who choose to follow them and perform at a high level. This requires advanced leaders to be great communicators, excellent listeners, tolerant, and above all, caring and respecting those who work beneath them.

For advanced leaders to develop and strengthen their influential skills, they must begin with the value that all human beings understand and deserve respect no matter what job level they are in the organization. In addition, they must recognize that those same human beings have different skills and intelligence that can bring value to the organization.

Influential leaders must be authentic, and in doing so, these leaders must develop and strengthen their own leadership credibility (see previously discussed in Chapter 3: Leadership Has to Have a Beginning, in the Four Fundamental Approach). Of course, there are courses and seminars for guiding individuals, specifically in this subject matter, and perhaps it may offer some insightful information. Ultimately though, advanced leaders should develop their own method and style that fits their character. (*Case in point: Consider Mahatma Gandhi and Abraham Lincoln, two very influential leaders, with vastly different styles. Gandhi was known to be soft-spoken with an extraordinary ability to reason, while Lincoln was known to be a great speaker with a commanding presence. Not only both had positively impacted humanity, but they influenced generations of future leaders in all areas.*) In short, great leadership depends highly on being influential, but achieving it will be an evolutionary journey throughout time.

Tactical Communication

Advanced leadership depends heavily on proper communications, and nothing is more damaging to a leader's credibility and reputation when he or she is perceived to say the wrong things. For instance, how many times have people heard leaders communicate improperly, in which they had to apologize for their statements, or make presumptuous comments that offend others, and/or in other cases where leaders make promises that later many discover were frivolous?

Improper and/or questionable statements must be avoided at all times and in all stages of leadership, from the beginning stages to the advanced stages. Yet, many will argue it is especially important to avoid improper and/or questionable comments in the advanced stages of leadership because, one, advanced leaders are held at higher expectation standards than the nonadvanced leaders. Two, throughout time, advanced leaders have developed and improved their communication skills, and on many occasions have learned from their past mistakes. Lastly, advanced leaders' miscommunication can have a larger negative impact on the organization as a whole, in difference to those in a nonadvanced leadership role, in which their miscommunication can be damaging in certain areas of the organization.

Naturally, avoiding any miscommunication is central to leadership, and to do so, leaders must learn to become a tactical communicator.

Tactical communication refers to the ability to be conscious, intentional, unreactive, and thoughtful with statements made.

Being Conscious

To be conscious is to be aware of every statement made in various settings. For example, on many occasions, leaders have to speak to different groups of employees, management, or perhaps individuals outside the organization. In such situations, leaders must be prepared on the topics, issues and prospective issues for each group meeting, or in some occasions, individual meetings. Preparing in advance allows the leader to carefully craft their statement and consciously avoid any communication that might be perceived improper for each specific setting.

Being Intentional

To be intentional is to be mindful for every comment made. Take for example speech preparations, it requires attentiveness to every statement point in the speech. Similarly, with intentional communications, leaders must apply the same attentiveness during meetings and interactions with others. Whether it be for internal organizational announcement to all employees, or external announcement for those who work outside of the organization, leaders must be exact in the language they use, even if at times the language is intended to be general in nature.

Being Unreactive

To be unreactive is to be able to control an emotional response. Often, leaders are questioned and, at times, challenged by others in various speaking venues, in which leaders feel obligated to quickly respond. Unfortunately, on some occasions, this will lead to an improper emotional reaction comment(s), which later warrants an apology by these leaders. In such situations, leaders must consciously pause before responding, as they control their emotions and allow their rational minds to formulate an adequate response.

Being Thoughtful

To be thoughtful is to be considerate to the feelings of others. This approach necessitates the ability to be empathetic and sympathetic while communicating with others. For instance, if an employee or a group of employees have faced a hardship event, their leader must address this unfortunate incident by being understanding and sympathetic with regard to their experience. Moreover, thoughtful comments are not limited to hardship situations; in fact, thoughtful comments should be utilized regularly as a positive reinforcement in the workplace. The more leaders recognize their staff for specific accomplishments through pleasant remarks, the more the staff is motivated to continue their good work and improve.

Public Persona

Rarely discussed in advanced leadership training is the importance of public persona of leaders. Public persona refers to the public image or character presented by a person, or in this case, by a leader (Chard 2013). What leaders show and how they show it to the public is the reflection of the organization they are representing. For example, the late Steve Jobs would present Apple's latest product on the stage in front of many in a very casual attire, which is reflective of the culture of a forward-thinking technology company. On the other hand, leaders of other industries might present themselves in a formal manner that reflects their organization's culture and mission.

The most important factor is that leaders must present themselves in a positive way, as on many occasions, leaders are judged by their public image rather than their actual achievements, which at times creates public controversies. Such as, if a highly successful athlete makes disparaging statements toward his or her fans during public appearances and interviews, that athlete's public image would be tarnished and would shadow his or her contribution to the sport. On the opposite side, even if an athlete was unsuccessful in his or her sport but is known to be charitable, tactful, and considerate to others, his or her public image would certainly be a positive one, especially as a representative of his or her sport. Ideally though, a leader's achievements should overlap with their public image so that it would only strengthen the leader's integrity.

Public persona development may require the assistance of public image consultants, although it may not be necessary if leaders develop their own methods. To do so, it will take a *Conscious Thought Approach* and a *Conscious Effort to Create an Image* that is reflective of the leader's personality and accomplishments.

A *Conscious Thought Approach* is the process of being mindful and self-aware of every public behavior action taken, which combines body language communication (which essentially is *Nonverbal Communication* by one's body or facial expression that reveals certain emotions) and tactical communication, as we discussed previously in Tactical Communication section. Merged with *Conscious Effort to Create an Image* (which essentially is leaders purposely envisioning their public image) would in fact allow leaders to develop and/or improve their public persona.

(*Case in point: A small business owner built a successful company from 5 to 500 employees throughout the years. Her business accomplishments are clearly evident, and while she fostered a good reputation as a strong business-person, she did not have any public presence. Understanding the importance of public appearances, she began developing her own public persona by combining her personal values and professional business qualities with her human side, while strategically preparing for public communications, with the anticipation of challenging questions. In time, she was able to create a strong public image for both herself and as a representative of the company.*)

This hypothetical situation is an example of how leaders can develop their own public persona, and while the process may sound simple, it does require planning, execution, and above all, discipline to maintain this process.

Decisiveness

By now, everyone understands, or should understand, that being a leader requires the ability to make decisions, especially during critical situations. Yet, often we have seen those in advanced leadership roles are too hesitant to make a decision and require lots of data, information, and opinions from other professionals. Or on the other side, there are those leaders who are quick to decide without thinking about the issues thoroughly. Certainly, both of these approaches are not ideal; in fact, they can both be detrimental. If a leader takes too long to make a decision and fails to do so during critical times, the results might be damaging. On the other hand, if a leader decides too fast, it can also have damaging effects.

It is important for leaders in all stages to be able to make sound, reasonable, and timely decisions based on the information, facts, and data they currently possess. However, on many occasions, leaders are faced with difficult decision-making scenarios in which the information, facts, and data are limited. In these types of situations, leaders must consider each decision and conceivably balance the positive outcomes versus the negative outcomes with each decision before committing to it. In another word, if the decision has a 70 to 90 percent likely positive result with a 10 to 30 negative result, that decision would be considered a good decision simply because of a higher percentage of success, even though, the decision does not have 100 percent positive outcomes.

Many who entered leadership have discovered that decision making is one of the most difficult tasks of any leader, and the more advanced the leader is, the more difficult decisions can become. With advanced leadership roles, leaders are faced with decisions that may have a larger impact on a larger group of people, which can result in higher accountabilities if the decision(s) are damaging enough. However, leaders should not dread taking reasonable steps to decide on issues that are in the gray areas, especially since real issues of life are never black and white.

Accomplishing Objectives Without Overwhelming Staff

Generally, leaders are expected to achieve their objectives with the assistance of their staff, yet, on most occasions, it is never a smooth process. Either, the leader may have accepted or created goals that are difficult to achieve during a certain period of time, or the high turnover of key staff members created difficulties to fulfill reasonable goals that were previously set. Yet often, in such circumstances, leaders continue to push their staff to accomplish these goals without changing the deadlines or resetting objectives that are more reasonable. Of course, in time, the staff may accomplish these goals under adverse conditions; however, this pace cannot continue as a standard working day because eventually staff will experience extreme fatigue that may cause illness, or the staff will eventually resign from their current roles.

In these type of situations, advanced leaders must develop their own methods of balancing their objectives with the staff's regular workdays, with some exceptions. The key is to be able to distinguish between the exceptional situations from the normal everyday situations. Still, it is true, that on many occasions, leaders and their staff must complete urgent matters in a timely fashion, and, of course, will require staff to work outside of their normal practices. These types of situations are considered the exceptions but not necessarily the rule, simply because, while many leaders may argue that every task is important, it does not mean that every task is urgent.

Distinguishing between important and urgent projects from important and nonurgent projects is a principle that advanced leaders should understand and practice in order to create a balance between completing projects and underwhelming staff. Ideally, leaders should be able to divide the important and urgent projects from the important and nonurgent ones by prioritizing each project from the most important to the least important. However, leaders should be cautious that the percentage of important and urgent projects does not outweigh the percentage of important and nonurgent projects; in other words, the ratio should not be 70 percent important-urgent and 30 percent important-nonurgent, rather it should be the opposite.

Leaders must also be willing to be flexible with time-managing projects with their teams. Too often, many projects are delayed by unforeseen events and may not be completed in a timely fashion. In such situations, leaders must evaluate whether overtime work for their team is necessary or should leaders adjust the deadline and set reasonable project completion expectations.

In the past, leaders that were driven by completing projects with no thought of being flexible (when it is optional) only created a harsh work environment that turnover staff. Yet, with the lessons of time, advanced leaders learned that their success cannot be achieved without the help of their staff and cannot be achieved by overdriving them to work overtime as part of their normal routine. The ability to be reasonable and flexible is a strong trait of advanced leaders, and those who adopt this thought process have not only created a team environment but they also succeeded.

Future Planning

It is the responsibility of any leader in the advanced stage of leadership to be able to plan for the future, whether one is a CEO or a departmental leader. The future of an organization relies heavily on the leader of the organization to strategize for the continuous operational success of that organization. Whether an organization is a profit-driven or a nonprofit institution, they must maintain their success for generations to come. Similarly, department leaders must have the same mindset as CEOs to be able to plan for the future of their department for its continuous operations.

In general, future planning is the ability to anticipate future business and/or needs for the organization and its departments. That being so, planning has various steps, and no one exact method is more effective than the other. However, before one begins to plan for the future, one should have a clear understanding of the following:

1. An understanding of what makes the organization or the department overall successful—from production to a collaborative work environment.
2. An understanding of the main elements of past and current success, including any failures during the process.
3. An understanding of the lessons that are learned during the process of past successes and failures, in order to determine future actions and behavior.

Still, even with knowledge of past successes and/or failures, advanced leaders must be able to anticipate new or additional needs for the organization in order to further strive in the future. CEOs and their organizational leaders must strategize together, utilizing various methods to create a comprehensive organizational strategy for the future of the organization. In addition, departmental leaders must tailor their departmental strategy to the organization's future strategies in furtherance of achieving the future objectives of the establishment.

Work Within Multifunctional Teams

A functioning organization has many facets to its operations, from the actual mechanics that operate it to the people, finances, and technology that help make it a successful organization. Naturally, there are many teams with different functions who must work together in order to operate successfully. Each team will have one departmental leader that must partner with another departmental leader to help further the organization's objectives, often referred to as cross-functional teams (Organ 2022). Of course, as the old expression held—easier said than done.

One of the main internal problems that organizations face throughout the years is a lack of departmental collaborations for various reasons, whether it be personality conflicts, values differences, ego, socially unacceptable behaviors, and so on. Certainly, there are different solutions to these problems, and many of them can be successful, but rather than focusing on resolving potential or existing conflicts, adopting a proactive approach to avoid such issues is ideal in most cases.

Historically speaking, there have been advanced leaders who managed to accomplish and overcome many challenges, and it was not achieved by their own efforts alone, rather, it was accomplished by partnering with other advanced leaders and learning to work with other leaders with different personalities, different work habits, and functions. Of course, there are times when a particular leader desires partnership with other leaders and received little cooperation, which at that point, he or she must become a leader of leaders and help drive the organization's goals.

The leader must consistently reinforce the organizational goals and its significant impact that will have to the overall organization's success. Adopt project management strategies by designing a plan of action with specified timelines. Facilitate each meeting to ensure that items on the project(s) are timely completed while simultaneously planning the next phase of the project(s) until the project(s) are completed.

In addition, a leader should develop or strengthen his or her professional relationship with other leaders through common personal interests, whether it be similar activities, values, or anything that would build friendship and comradery in the workplace. These relationships are critical for improving the overall culture of the organization and the overall productivity. However, it takes a courageous leader to initiate these relationships, and on many occasions, the path to such relationships is never unchallenging; nonetheless, the leader has to be hopeful, patient, and rational. To paraphrase President Barack Obama, "I will extend my hand if you are willing to unclench your fist," is the mindset that leaders must have (Obama 2009).

Multifaceted Mindset

In various professional industries, successful leaders have learned to think outside their trained professions; whether the leader's profession is a doctor or an engineer, these leaders began developing a multifaceted mindset that allowed them to be successful.

A multifaceted mindset is the ability to think through various disciplines or functions without limiting it to one's trained profession. (*Case in point: A doctor who is in a leadership role must manage staff, work with other departments (as discussed previously), and, on occasion, have budgetary responsibilities, plan for the future of the department, and so on. Therefore, this doctor cannot be limited to patient care functions and responsibilities.*)

A multifaceted mindset is usually developed during the first stages of leadership training or on many occasions through daily practice as a supervisor, manager, or other positions in leadership. In such circumstances, these new leaders find themselves in situations that compel them to perform their job beyond their trained profession (as described in the previous example) and if not, they will ultimately fail as leaders. Naturally, the successful leaders adapt to learning new and different ideas from various professions, while discovering some of their overall strengths and weaknesses as leaders.

Good leadership is an evolutionary process, and during this process, leaders must make a conscious effort to think through different disciplines by learning the basics of each discipline; for example, if a leader is the head of an accounting department, he or she must understand the basics of human resources, information technology, public relations, industry business, and so on. As the old cliché goes, leaders must wear different hats for different occasions, and in any leadership role, this is a must in order to be successful.

PHASE 5

The Fourth Stage—
The Practice

CHAPTER 10

The Practice

Great leadership is an ongoing process, but more importantly, it is an evolutionary process, as mentioned in Concluding the First Stage section. Many great leaders will acknowledge their failures and successes during this evolutionary process and have learned many lessons along the way. One important lesson that seems to be echoed by many leaders is the ability to be strategic in all forms of leadership, and not necessarily be limited to operational strategies, especially when it pertains to relating to human beings.

Approach to Managing Staff

It is common knowledge that within every industry, there are many different types of people in the workforce, with different personalities, cultural diversities, professions, intelligence, skill levels, and motivations. For leaders, to assume that there is only one all-purpose method for managing staff is unrealistic, even though, there are those who prefer a one-style method and believe that it can be effective. In general, there are certain industries that might have similar cultures and similar staff behaviors in which a one-style method might be effective; however, in most industries, with a significant amount of diversity in their workforce, the success of a one-style method application is not likely.

In Chapter 2: Brief History of Leadership Theories, this book describes various ideas and principles for proper leadership capabilities. Many of these principles have redeeming qualities that are well-researched and well-written; however, rarely all of these principles and theories are ideal for every personality and situation. Naturally, it stands to reason, given the fact that human behaviors are complex, and it is difficult to create a standard leadership principle that fits all personalities and situations. Furthermore, these principles seldom focus on creating and building the core competencies needed to be a leader (see Phase 2: The First Stage—The Genesis of a leader), to which these principles can properly be applied.

Through years of practice, great leaders discovered that they must approach managing staff with a variety of styles and mindsets. While one approach might work for some, it might not work with others, and it is that discovery that allowed great leaders to be versatile when leading different personalities and in different situations.

Of course, no experienced great leader or expert leadership trainer can describe every personality and situation by which certain styles of leadership can apply. Even though there are leadership trainers who created their own hypothetical situations to illustrate the application of certain leadership principles, and in certain circumstances, it can be helpful. However, in most occasions, it is too difficult to imagine every possible scenario to apply these leadership principles, so therefore, leaders have to rely on their foundational leadership skills, coupled with the versatility mindset that allows them to manage different personalities in different situations.

Cultivating Relationships

For staff to be guided effectively, there must be good relations between the staff and their leaders, and in such situations, it is the responsibility of the leaders to nurture such relationships. Many staff turnovers, leadership complaints, and dysfunctional teams were attributed to failed relations between staff and their leaders, and yet when these leaders discover the reasons for staff dissatisfaction, many of these leaders are usually surprised (Jabli 2022). Partly, because these leaders have never developed a good working relationship that encompasses regular and honest communication exchange with their staff, rather the communication is usually unilateral by which the leader speaks while the staff listens. Other reasons might be a lack of daily, weekly, or even monthly interactions between leaders and their staff. Regardless of the reasons, leaders have to develop and cultivate relations with their staff.

There are two factors to consider when developing relations with staff: (1) the professional business relations, in which the roles are clearly defined (i.e., staff and supervisor); and (2) the human relations factor that helps create a more personal connection between the staff and their supervisors. This relationship can be summarized with a few fundamental social behaviors that are suited in the workplace:

- Respecting every staff member.
- Caring for the staff member's well-being.
- Assist staff to excel with their career objectives.
- And above all, allow staff accessibility to listen to them individually or collectively.

However, cultivating this relationship is not easy, simply because, leaders must balance a level of friendliness, professionalism, and thoughtfulness but without intruding in their staff's personal and private life. For example, if a staff member confides to his or her supervisor that there was a death in the family, it would be appropriate for that supervisor (in accordance with the organization's policy and practice) to send a card and flowers to the staff member's home. Yet, if this staff member confides to his or her supervisor personal information that a reasonable person might find unprofessional, offensive, or anything socially unacceptable, this supervisor must not continue this conversation with this staff member and gracefully explain the reasons for discontinuing this topic(s).

Most individuals spend 40 hours or more a week at work, more time than they spend with their loved ones and close friends, so it would stand to reason that work relations between staff and their leaders must be developed and nurtured in order to create a great work environment and great culture, and it is the leader's responsibility to create it and manage it.

Partnership

The concept of partnership is one of the easiest concepts to understand, yet it seems to be one of the most difficult to practice, especially by leaders. Many leaders understand partnership with other leaders, but rarely do they ever think about partnering up with their staff; the main reason is because they view this relationship as the boss over his or her subordinate's associations by which the boss commands while the employee performs her or his duties. This usually falls under a more authoritative style of leadership that is only effective in limited circumstances. The idea of leaders partnering with their staff began organically by what some believe through the practice of empowering their staff to do the best they can in order to build their confidence. The more staff were empowered, the more they became successful and valued experts in their job, and the more leaders began to treat them as partners rather than subordinates. Yet, partnership should be part of all employee's and their leader's daily practice, and in order for this to occur, leaders must create a partnership culture for the entire organization.

Like other positive work behaviors, partnership behavior is no different than any other positive behavior; it is a behavior that has no disadvantages, but it must be regularly practiced and reinforced by leaders. The more leaders incorporate partnership principles with their teams and others in the organization, the more it becomes part of the culture. This principle has been proven successful for many organizations that have committed themselves to creating a great work environment and lengthy employee retention.

Building Teams

For leaders, creating an effective team is the second most challenging task next to rebuilding a dysfunctional team, which will be discussed in the next category. On many occasions, building a team can be stressful and taxing because it is not as simple as hiring anyone to fill one of the positions for a forthcoming team, especially, if the team-to-be consists of skilled professionals. To create an effective team, leaders should consider the following methods: Analysis, Vision, Strategy, and Execution, combined with Flexibility.

Analysis

Before recruiting talent for the team, leaders must analyze and identify the technical skills needed for their department or their organization. For example, startup companies are usually led by their founder and CEO, and during the beginning stages of the company, the CEO will identify the operational and administrative talent needed for business operations. This might require creating a corporate structure by hiring departmental leaders in operations, finance, human resources, compliance, and so on.

Yet, for each department of the organization, departmental leaders will analyze and identify the right technical skills that are needed to support the organization's overall goals. For instance, the head of finance might hire an accounting specialist, such as someone that have tax expertise, if the organization's business regularly deals with tax matters.

Vision

Whether leaders are the heads of organizations or departmental leaders, every leader should have an ideal vision of how their organization or department functions. From workforce productivity to proper staff behavior, which is usually subjective, given the fact that most leaders desire individuals that will complement their leadership style. For example, those who lead by authority might desire staff that only follow instructions; however, those who lead by influence will likely want a staff that can be motivated by positive thinking and so on. Therefore, it is important for leaders to understand their own leadership style and approach to managing staff when considering behavior compatibilities.

The leader's vision should include a reasonable expectation of a short-term as well as a long-term departmental or organizational accomplishment once the team is created. Yet, more importantly, the short-term plan should be designed as a segment leading to the long-term plan, or another view point, the short-term plan is designed to be the foundation for the long-term plan.

Strategy and Execution

After analyzing the necessary skills and behavior needed for the organization or the department and creating a vision of how the organization and department will ideally function, the next major step is to strategically recruit and hire the individuals for the organization or department. First, job descriptions should be created for all the positions that are needed. Second, prioritize the most important skills to the least important skills needed for each position. Third, if the position(s) is entry-level, then leaders must identify those with the core skills that can be trained and developed into seasoned professionals. And fourth, begin the recruitment process utilizing whatever recruiting method is available. *Important note: During the process of creating a job description, be sure that the skills and experiences listed are realistic and not idealistic from a hiring perspective. (Case in point: If a leader is recruiting for an engineer position and is requiring the engineer to be certified in both civil and electrical [which might be ideal in some industries], the probability of finding more than one candidate in the United States would be extremely low.)*

Flexibility

Many experienced leaders understand during the team-building process that they must be able to be flexible with their staff requirements. On many occasions, while recruiting for the ideal candidates, seldom leaders ever find such candidates for various reasons. For instance, if a leader is recruiting local candidates in order to have them work at the location of the organization and discovers that most candidates reside out of the state, this leader should consider being flexible to either modifying his or her job requirements or allow for remote work with some travel or consider other alternatives to this challenge. Most importantly, the leader should not wait too long for the ideal candidates, instead, allow reasonable time for the recruitment process to work before making any changes. Of course, a reasonable time is subjective given the fact that there are some positions that are necessary for the organization, and it is not unusual for leaders to continue to recruit for over a year.

Rebuilding Teams

On many occasions, leaders accept new positions in other organizations that have existing teams that were created by the previous leaders. This can be very positive if the teams are efficient and overall meet the general efficiency standard by the new leaders. However, imagine the contrary, that a leader discovers that the team he or she inherited is dysfunctional in various ways, from a lack of skill competencies and an uncollaborative environment to a lack of motivation, which is a common scenario in the workplace.

Naturally, the success of this leader depends on the efficiency of the team, and this leader understands that he or she must rebuild the team to be more efficient without terminating any member of the team and replacing others. Doing so requires an in-depth analysis of the reasons for such inefficiencies. It might be a combination of several issues, such as a lack of training resources to enhance their technical skills, team members not working within their strength, rather being tasked to do other duties, and/or a lack of motivation due to poor leadership and so on.

Thereafter, the leader should create a strategic plan to address and improve the areas of his or her team's deficiencies. However, all leaders should know that there is not one exact plan to do so; in fact, leaders will discover that they might apply different strategies to different team members. Nonetheless, leaders can begin with a foundational approach by devising an inclusive departmental or organizational plan that requires the participation of each team member, simultaneously inspiring and empowering them to be significantly instrumental in reaching the goals that are set by the plan.

If the plan implementation is successful due to the team's contribution, then it is a considerable improvement of a dysfunctional team. However, if during the execution of this plan, it appears that success will not be achieved, the leaders (at minimum) would discover and curtail some of the team's limitations and try to find a solution(s), such as readjusting the plan by working the strength of each team member and allowing them to contribute in the best of their abilities.

As mentioned previously, there is no exact way of rebuilding a team, and it is not a simple task, but past successful leaders found that they had to be patient, regularly try to motivate their staff, and consider different ideas and approaches to enhance the team, and more importantly, analyze and address the core issues that are holding the staff from becoming efficient.

Creating a Culture

Every organization that employs people, whether it be a business corporation, nonprofit, government, or small business, have a culture. Whether that culture is weak or strong would depend on the overall viewpoint of the employees. The culture of an organization is a set of behaviors and values that are driven by the leaders through their policies, procedures, communication, standard of conduct, and overall treatment of their employees. When the culture is weak, it will be evidenced by many factors, such as conflicts among employees and/or their managers, lack of cooperation among management, high employee turnovers, and/or employee-related litigations. On the other hand, when the culture is strong, it is exactly the opposite, and it can be shown by the employee retention rate, lack of conflicts among employees and management within the organization, an increase in work quality, more confident employees, and a high rate of employee participations and engagements (Srinivasan and Kurey 2014).

Culture Creation or Culture Improvements must be led and managed by the leaders of the organization; in fact, one leader cannot change the culture of the organization by themselves, rather a leader can only affect the culture of his or her team.

Culture Creation

Normally, creating a culture usually occurs during the startup phase of the organization if certain steps are taken by the leadership of that origination. First, leaders must list culture as the top priority for their organization. Second, leaders must visualize the ideal culture for their organization. Third, leaders must define the specific behaviors that would support the vision of the culture. Fourth, leaders must incorporate those desired cultural behaviors into their mission and value statement. Lastly, leaders must formalize their cultural behaviors by adding it to their policies and procedures of the organization.

Culture Improvements

The necessity for culture improvements is usually driven by a noticeable negative culture within the organization. This typically occurs in existing organizations which either did not create a good culture from the start of the organization, or throughout the years, organizations had incorporated bad leadership that were instrumental in damaging the organization's culture.

Improving the culture of an organization can be very challenging, and very time-consuming, yet highly important. The process begins with the leader of the organization and his or her team identifying the key negative behavior elements that are affecting the culture of the organization, strategies for a solution, and creating an action plan. For example, if the negative behaviors are ethically related, the leader and his or her team must create a strong ethical policy, coupled with ethical training, followed by a means for accountability. More importantly, leaders must continue to reinforce ethical behavior and practice with all the teams of the organization. In time, the negative behavior in the culture will eventually diminish, and culture improvement will be clearly noticeable to everyone in the organization.

Organic Culture Changes

Changes in the culture can occur organically through new team members, new leadership, and/or new leaders of the organization. However, these changes can have a negative or a positive impact on the organization, depending on the type of effect these new hires have on the organization. For example, if these new hires are driven by success, yet lack the ability to collaborate with other team members, it might create distrust and unruliness among the team, which ultimately will affect the culture negatively. On the other hand, if these new hires are driven to succeed through collaboration and respect for other team members, the effect on the culture of the organization will be positive.

To avoid any negative aspects of organic culture changes, it must begin during the recruitment process. Besides skills and qualifications, leaders must evaluate each qualified candidate for a culture fit by asking proper behavior questions during the interview process. After the selection process is completed and individuals are hired, leadership must orientate the new hires on the mission, values, and culture of the organization and continuously reinforce these behavior ideas throughout time.

Departmental or Team Culture

Most professionals rarely think about culture within their department and/or team. Usually, culture is believed to be the collective behavior of the organization as a whole, and naturally, it is believed that these behaviors are transmitted into the departments and/or teams. In most cases, this belief is correct; however, there are circumstances in which the behavior of the department or team leader contradicts the organization's culture in various ways that ultimately result in confusion and other negative effects among staff. In addition, it can ultimately compromise the overall organizational culture if the behaviors are not corrected.

For example, if the current culture of the organization is based on great communication, collaboration, respect, employee empowerment, fairness, and overall great ethics, yet one of the department leaders' behaviors is contrasting the organizational culture, in the manner that he or she communicates poorly with staff, does not encourage collaboration rather creates hostility among staff, consistently favoring some over others, and overall unethical conduct. Clearly, these behaviors are unacceptable and must be corrected because the consequences at minimum will be low morale, high turnovers, conflicts between staff, and so on.

For organizations to maintain great cultures, they must rely heavily on the participation of all departments and team leaders. If one or more departments or teams fail to participate, the organization's culture is compromised, given the fact that an organization cannot have collective behaviors (culture) if part of the organization is behaving differently, or worse, contradicting.

Lastly, creating, changing, and/or maintaining culture can be very challenging if organizational leaders neglect to prioritize culture as an important element in their strategic goals, mission, and values.

The Fifth Stage— A Leader of Leaders

CHAPTER 11

Leader of Leaders

As advanced leaders evolve in their leadership roles, they will eventually have the opportunity to lead other leaders. This is an area that is rarely discussed in leadership topics, yet highly important, given the fact that leading leaders is unlike managing staff.

In essence, a leader of leaders is someone in a higher-level leadership role, such as a CEO, who leads other less-ranking leaders, such as department heads. Of course, a leader of leaders can also apply to departmental leaders and less-ranking leaders as long as they are leading others who are in leadership roles, such as directors, managers, supervisors, and so on (Salacuse 2006).

During this stage of leadership, higher-ranking leaders must recognize that these lower ranking leaders are not junior staff members who will need guidance, mentorship, or worse, micromanagement and assigned duties. Instead, higher-ranking leaders must be able to distinguish their leadership approach between their lower-ranking leaders and their junior staff members.

Distinctions and Approach

To distinguish between junior staff members from lower-ranking leaders, advanced leaders must consider their job needs. As mentioned in Empowering Individuals, junior staff members need guidance, mentorship, training, teaching, assigned duties, and overall management. On the other hand, lower-ranking leaders do not need to be managed, rather they need to be led by empowerment and influence, given clear directions, and most importantly, allow them to make decisions that they will be accountable for all decisions.

(*Note*: On occasions, lower-ranking leaders may need development into a higher level of leadership role, which will require a one-on-one discussion between the higher-ranking leader and the lower-ranking leader. In this discussion, the higher-ranking leader with the collaboration of the lower-ranking leader devises a development plan and set expectations.)

In previous years, successful advanced leaders have adopted the concept of partnership with their lower-ranking leaders. As such, they created a working environment that allows full participation in strategic meeting sessions and a say on decisions that usually affect the organization without being fully democratic, in which leaders will have voting rights on the final decisions. The main reason is that the higher-ranking leader alone will be held accountable for his or her decisions regardless of the decision's outcome. Furthermore, partnership requires a significant amount of trust in the skills and abilities of the lower-ranking leaders, given the fact that they have earned their leadership role by past accomplishments and success in their previous roles. Still, higher-ranking leaders must have a clear understanding of their lower-ranking leader's abilities and skills in order to set proper project result expectations. As such, that will require that the higher-ranking leader utilize their overall strengths and capabilities during project partnerships.

For the lower-ranking leaders, they must understand that this partnership is a bilateral relationship with the higher-ranking leader, which requires the same trust, respect, and professional collaboration. Yet, while many leaders have embraced this partnership concept, there are other leaders who have rejected it, simply because some believe that this concept will relinquish some of their authority, and they will not be able to lead properly. However, this belief is not substantiated by any facts, rather this belief is more of a concern for those who rely on an authority style of leadership.

Incorporating the Mission and Values in the Organizational Objectives

The mission of the organization is the primary reason for the existence of an organization; it defines the organization's purpose and overall aim. The values of the organization are the leading principles that provide an organization with its cultural roots. These two components are truly the heart of the organization, and they should always be introduced to new employees and reinforced to the current employees.

It starts with the higher-ranking leader as he or she designs and defines the objectives for the organization by incorporating the mission of the organization as the main purpose to fulfill while creating an action plan that is aligned with the values of the organization.

(*Case in point: Assuming there is an organization in the renewable energy industry and its mission is to produce environmentally friendly energy sources. Clearly, their operational objectives would be focused on solar, wind, and so on. However, if this organization utilized nonenvironmentally friendly sources, such as coal and/or gas, it would contradict and defeat its mission. Similarly, if the values of this organization are ethically driven by the purpose of the mission and general ethical behavior, setting objectives that are contrary to the mission violates the organization's values.*)

In addition, the higher-ranking leader must set expectations for his or her lower-ranking leaders to follow the same method of incorporating the mission and values into departmental or team objectives. It is only then that the organization can operate concurrently and harmoniously.

Organization's Representatives

Clearly, the CEO or higher-ranking leader of the organization is typically known as the "face of the organization" simply because he or she represents the organization in both areas, externally and internally. Specifically, external representation is for the general public, while internal is representation for the employee populations.

For many Boards of Directors (to whom the CEO reports), this is a very important duty as they hold the CEO accountable for how he or she represents the organization. On many occasions, the CEO will represent the organization in a positive manner to fulfill the mission of the organization, while avoiding any controversies. Similarly, departmental leaders are expected to do the same since they are considered the "face of their department." However, it is the responsibility of the leader of leaders (CEO) to empower his or her departmental leaders to represent their departments in the same fashion as the CEO, in a positive manner that furthers the organization's mission.

Representation

Some might question the reason for departmental leaders representing the organization, given the fact that most public appearances are performed by the CEO. Still, on many occasions, departmental leaders have and continuously attend work-related public conferences, from industry-specific conferences to occupation-specific summits, such as for accounting, human resources, legal, and so on.

(*Case in point: During these conferences, the Chief Financial Officer [CFO] might be asked specific questions about the organization that may not necessarily be financially related, but in the absence of the CEO, the CFO must answer every question the same as the CEO. Certainly, the same approach applies to all other departmental leaders, so it is imperative to be prepared for public appearances, even if there is less likelihood that the public will ask questions about the organization.*)

There are two main elements of departmental leadership representations: (1) representation on behalf of the organization; and (2) representation of the department of the organization, both externally and internally. For public appearances, departmental leaders must prepare to answer questions the same as the CEO, so it is important to have a unified message to the public, regardless of the topic. On the other hand, for internal representation to the employee population, the approach is the same in the matter of being positive and noncontroversial, yet different since departmental leaders are only representing their department. While each department shares one common purpose, and that is to support the goals and mission of the organization, their support functions for the organization differ from one to another.

In the case of the leader of the finance department, the CFO is responsible for internal and external financial reports. Internally, the CFO must report financial matters not only to the board but also to the employee population of the organization as well. With public reporting, the CFO may do the same type of reporting (depending on the situation), but usually, the financial reporting for the public is much broader than the board report.

Lastly, at all levels of leadership, representing the organization is a responsibility that falls within the duties of leadership. Higher-ranking leaders must ensure that this practice is embedded in the culture and values of the organization to maintain and strengthen external and internal relations.

Leadership is an evolutionary process with no limit to its progress even by the time a person becomes a leader of leaders. Certainly, at this stage of leadership, it is the highest level of management in the workplace; nonetheless, the learning and development of becoming a great leader never stops. The more experience leading a diverse workforce in various situations, the more lesson learned, and the more likelihood of becoming a great leader.

PHASE 7

The Sixth Stage—
The Journey

CHAPTER 12

The Journey of Leadership

At last, the journey begins for new leaders, and for existing leaders, the journey has already begun. For both, new and existing leaders, their journey might have similarities, but in most cases, their journey experience will be vastly different. Yet, individuals should understand that their leadership journey began long before they became leaders. It actually started when they became employees and were led by an individual who might have been a supervisor, manager, or anyone else in a leadership role.

During this experience, individuals discover the feeling of being managed by another person, and for many, they will have good and/or bad experiences, depending on how they were led. If one would ask most seasoned good leaders to reflect on their career and the reason for their leadership success, many might attribute it to a great leader that they have learned from, even though these same leaders might attribute their leadership success to the bad leaders that they were exposed to throughout the years.

Exposure to bad leadership has been known to teach new leaders as to "what not to do"; in fact, there are many good leaders who will say that because of bad leadership experiences, they have learned to be more thoughtful and intentional while leading others. Consequently, whether the experiences have been positive or negative, there are learning lessons in all of them, as long as one does not subconsciously adopt the negative traits of bad leadership.

Lessons From Mistakes

Mistakes will eventually happen in one's leadership journey, and usually, these mistakes will differ from one leader to another, and from one issue(s) to another. Yet throughout the years, we have seen common mistakes traits by leaders during their leadership journey that with proper conscious effort can be avoided.

Being a Boss

One of the most common scenarios during a time when individuals are embarking on their first leadership role is the tendency and the desire to demonstrate that they are the "boss" to their staff. By taking a commanding role and making changes prematurely before evaluations, at the same time, tasking and micromanaging the staff without properly explaining the reasons for the tasked projects.

In the last decade or so, the notion of being a "boss" is no longer welcomed in the workplace; in fact, there are numerous publications that promote "being a leader" rather than "being a boss," mainly because history has shown us that being a boss has a limited time of effectiveness while leading others has an unlimited time of effectiveness. The main difference is the mindset; a boss has a ruling or governing mentality, while a leader has a leading, motivating, and influencing mentality. Again, time has shown us that human beings in the workplace respond to leadership and not to bosses, which supports the long-standing number one reason for people leaving their jobs, and that is because of their boss. Yet, year after year, many leaders begin their leadership journey by attempting to be the boss, with all the studies and information that are available online, bookstores, and so on.

But in time, good leaders do emerge from this practice when they realize that during the period when they were bosses, it was failed leadership and the lessons that rose out of this phase that contributed to existing good leadership.

Perception of Intellectual Arrogance

Throughout time, many leaders have been perceived as being intellectually arrogant in their daily interactions with their staff and colleagues. Usually, this perception comes from a very self-assured, outspoken, and somewhat commanding presence leader, yet, with the inability to listen to others, especially those who are subordinates to him or her. Combine additional bad behaviors, such as a superiority attitude, entitlement, and elitism, and this perception becomes a factual reality. To be clear, however, being self-assured, outspoken, and having a commanding presence alone should not be considered intellectually arrogant, but rather, more as being confident, especially when it is coupled with humility.

Being perceived as intellectually arrogant can be damaging to the overall credibility of a leader in several ways. No longer will staff be empowered to do their job and grow as professionals; at the same time, colleagues will less likely engage this leader with projects, unless it is necessary. Many attribute this behavior to a lack of emotional intelligence, vanity, and entitlement, and perhaps they are accurate on all accounts.

Still, those who have worked in the frontline of human resources have observed an additional bad behavior that contributes to this intellectual arrogance conduct, and it is *elitism by leadership job titles*. As some individuals that were newly hired or promoted to a leadership role and have obtained the titles of managers, directors, vice presidents, or CEOs, their behavior and attitude seem to change. Some have described it as: They begin as friendly professionals and transform into an arrogant, authority-driven individuals with superiority attitude. This seems to occur directly after advancing into a leadership role. One of the main signs of this behavior is when these leaders express the desire to be treated differently than those in nonleadership roles, such as with preferable treatment that would lead to greater benefits.

Elitism by leadership job titles is not uncommon in the workforce, yet, it is rarely discussed simply because no one understands the root cause of this behavior. Many can only speculate the origin of this behavior and attempt to find solutions for it, of course, if it is recognized. However, it would seem that the most effective method of avoiding it is to be conscious of this behavior as a leader and allow humility to overcome it.

Questionable Decisions

The journey of leadership will have countless decisions that will be made during one's career, and while every leader would like to make perfect decisions, it is unfortunately impossible. Nonetheless, one can limit bad decisions in one's career by evaluating all the steps that were taken, coupled with their emotions at the time the decision(s) was made, and learning from its mistake.

Emotions have always played a role in the decision-making process, both privately and professionally. If an individual is anxious, angry, and, overall, highly stressed, their reasoning will usually be compromised. Once the reasoning is compromised, the decision(s) will likely be made poorly, simply because the decision(s) was not thoughtfully and carefully considered with a rational mindset. Unfortunately, every leader at some instance in their career will make an irrational decision that would lead to an unsuccessful situation(s), but of course, as mentioned, such situations can be avoided by learning from past conduct and allowing reason to lead on all the decision-making processes.

Another component that can lead to questionable decisions is that of an overly ambitious goal that is driven by an individual vanity. Many leaders in the past have failed in their attempt to reach goals that most would consider excessively aggressive. (*Case in point: A CEO promises the board that by the following year, the company will show 30 percent growth, even though, the most the company had ever increased its growth in one year was approximately 5 percent. The probability of this CEO achieving that 30 percent is unlikely, which makes his or her goals overly aggressive.*)

Usually, this occurs with new leaders at all levels of management (although, the results of bad decisions may have a different impact on the company or staff depending on the level of leadership role that made such decision(s). Such that, a CEO's decision will affect the entire company, while a mid-level manager's decision(s) might impact a portion of the company).

Obviously, there are many more situations in which leaders can make questionable decisions during their leadership career, and unfortunately, it will happen to the best leaders, but the most important aspect of any questionable decisions is the learning lesson from it, and the ability to not repeat the mistake in the future.

Questionable Behaviors and Statements

Leaders are often in the public's eye, whether they are in front of their employees or the general public. During such situations, leaders are often scrutinized for every statement made and every questionable behavior, and while that might seem unfair to some leaders, others might view it differently. To employees and the general public, leaders are held to a higher standard of behavior than that of an average staff member in the organization, and it is, in fact, a part of the expectations of leadership. Yet, often leaders in various industries or public service have made inappropriate public statements and behaved unprofessionally, and for many of those leaders, they have regretted doing so.

Inappropriate statements can occur by mistake, or intentional, depending on the mindset of the leader at the time. For example, a mistaken inappropriate statement might be that of a stereotype remark about a person's heritage that could have been avoided if the leader had researched the subject matter before speaking. However, intentional inappropriate statements might be those that are heard by politicians during elections, in which, politicians resort to making derogatory remarks about their opponents, or some might refer to it as "trash talking" as they do sports entertainment. Unfortunately, some leaders in the workforce environment have resorted to the same methods with others in their organization or their competitors, and it is simply unprofessional.

On the other hand, questionable behavior is usually driven by an irrational mindset that at times might be severe enough that would warrant maximum disciplinary action; or in other times, it may be a minor infraction that raises questions about the leader's credibility. For example, expressing anger and belittling others, either verbally or in written form, and overall reacting to situations unreasonably, which could have been avoided, if one was in a rational mindset.

One of the measures of becoming a good leader is the ability to recognize current and past mistakes by identifying whether the mistake(s) are related to behavior, technical proficiencies, and/or operational decisions. By identifying the core of any mistake(s), a good leader should be able to make a conscious effort to correct the mistake(s) or avoid repeating it.

Successful Moments

As the journey continues for leaders, their experience will differ from one leader to another, as do their moments of success. At some point in a leader's career, he or she will have many successful times (of course, depending on how each leader defines his or her success). For example, some leaders define their success as several small wins throughout the year with various positive impacts, while others define their success as one significant win that has a sizeable positive impact. Regardless, it is important to recognize successful moments in this leadership journey, as it benefits others in the organization, strengthens the leader's confidence, and overall continues the motivation to thrive.

Of course, these successful moments never happened accidentally or randomly; in fact, success has always been intentional through proper planning. As individuals become leaders, they understand that there are objectives to be met from the first day on the job. These objectives can vary from building a team to furthering the business operations of the organization. But as time passes, many good leaders emerge, and many will have successful moments. Yet, in time, these leaders will discover that these successful moments are not easy to achieve, and while many leaders will plan for success, challenges during the process will occur. In such situations, leaders will either be discouraged and quit or face each challenge as it presents itself.

Still, there are certain common traits that many successful leaders share as they faced these challenges during the process of accomplishing their goals:

1. These leaders never lose sight of the main objectives.
2. They have a passion for accomplishing.
3. They maintain a professional and personal life balance.
4. They tend to have an optimistic view of life.
5. They apply Change Management: strategies when it is essential.
6. They adjust the process when it is crucial to overcome any challenges.
7. They maintain discipline and continue their efforts to accomplish their objectives.
8. Lastly, these leaders will celebrate and share their success with their team and emphasize their contribution with any successful moment(s).

Success and failures are part of the journey of leadership. Ideally, one should have more successes than failures throughout their career, yet this is not always the case. In the past, there have been many leaders who have failed more than they have succeeded, but by learning from their failures, they were able to succeed and make significant impacts. In other words, a successful moment that has a substantial effect can compensate for many small failures or mistakes, depending on the situation.

Maintaining Momentums

Accomplished leaders recognize that in order to succeed, they must continue to drive for success, and they must also stay in continual motion to accomplish such success. In other words, they must maintain momentums during their leadership journey, especially through challenging and stressful times.

Throughout this journey, many leaders might (and in most cases will) experience excessive stress and exhaustion during their management career due to various challenges. These challenges may begin to surface at the beginning of an individual's leadership stage; though, it will likely appear during the peak of his or her career. When such stress and exhaustion occur, it will have a negative effect on the individual's mindset and it will likely result in irrational actions that will eventually hamper short- and long-term success.

In recent years, many leaders have been able to recognize the onset of burning out and take steps to remedy it through various means, such as taking time off, maintaining work–life balance, and other available methods that fit the person's personality and their situation. However, maintaining strong leadership momentums throughout one's career (even with developing tolerance to burning out) can be challenging if the individual is unable to sustain constant motivation.

Certainly, being motivated consistently is not as simple as it seems, given the fact that there are many variables that can offset a motivated mind, such as mental health, life changes, stress, and so on. Nonetheless, past leaders have discovered that regardless of the challenges of life, the passion to achieve coupled with daily discipline allows for continuous motivations which ultimately maintain momentum throughout one's leadership career. Simply, **Momentum is [Passion + Discipline = Steady Motivations].**

Example scenario: As a new leadership team began to form a new organization, they understood that every organization has its life span; from its beginning (the startup stage) to the growth stage, leading to the stabilization or maturity stage. This process from the first stage to the last stage can be very lengthy and generally can take years to be achieved. In order to be successful, these leaders must continue their efforts through every stage of the organization while facing every challenge that life presents and somehow overcome it. In such situations, momentum is critical to drive the course of this entire process from the beginning stage to the desired long-term and final stage. And while not every leader will face this type of scenario, they will face other situations in which maintaining momentums must be applied to fulfill long-term objectives.

The Seventh and Final Stage

CHAPTER 13

The Author's Perspective

In the final stage of leadership, leaders should have evolved to become better and stronger leaders, with a higher level of expertise in their chosen profession, a clear understanding of human nature that applies to their proficiencies with human skills, and past ethical behavior, which can all be evidenced by their positive performance history.

During this period, there will be two types of leaders that will emerge: (1) The first type is a leader who is satisfied with his or her past achievements and look forward to the next phase of his or her life, which could mean preparing a successor so he or she can retire from the current role while starting a new role or retiring from all work. (2) The second type is a leader who is unsatisfied with their past accomplishments as if he or she has not accomplished enough or achieved the desired goals. Typically, this leader is driven to either accomplish more before retirement or create other opportunities to accomplish during retirement.

In any case, as these leaders face their final stage of leadership, many might begin to reflect on their careers and contemplate whether they had performed everything within their influence to help create a great work environment (whether it be for their team or the entire organization). And/or whether they had a strategy to share their gained knowledge through years of experience with the next generation of leaders. However, before leaders reflect on their past achievements, leaders must not overlook their current work environment and ask themselves whether they accomplished their objectives, and if it is not, consider the following checklist and make adjustments as needed.

Created a Great Work Environment

For seasoned leaders who have evolved to their last stage, this suggested 12 questions should be beneficial to make any adjustments that are needed. Keep in mind, that at any point in a leader's final stage, he or she can still make a significant impact on the team or the organization:

1. *Was the team or the organization productive and successful?* A few ways to think about productivity and success. First, quantitative results, which is the simplest method of establishing productivity and success. Second, progress through efforts, in which projectivity and foreseeable success can be established gradually.

2. *Were team members empowered to work their best?* Individual team members should have been able to contribute their ideas and be allowed to make mistakes, and some who have the ambitions to further their career are encouraged, motivated, and assisted by the leader to help further their career path.

3. *Was there training provided for the team to help their advancements?* Again, for those who have the desire to further their career, available training should have been provided, or at minimum, leaders could provide educational reimbursements to assist with their career objectives.

4. *Did the leader coach his or her team?* Coaching usually occurs in regular meetings, whether scheduled specifically for coaching or combined with other topics of discussion. Yet, the most important aspect of coaching is that leaders should have made a conscious effort to coach their individual team members. If there are circumstances in which leaders could not have coached their staff (as in the leading leader's situations), in that case, a leader must rely on influencing his or her leaders.

5. *Was the team encouraged to have a work–life balance?* Productive and happy individuals are those who have a balance between work and their private lives. Leaders must ensure that their team and/or organization include work–life balance as a part of their values and practice. Even though work–life balance has a different meaning for each employee, conceptually everyone understands that there has to be a separation between work and private life, and leaders must ensure that employees do not work past their normal period, unless during urgent situations.

6. *Were there collaborations among the team?* The overall success of a team is one method of confirming collaborations among them. However, on many occasions, even if teams fall short of success, their combined efforts can demonstrate their collaboration.

7. *Were there collaborations among departments?* While this question should be addressed by the head of the organization (since he or she is accountable for setting departmental teamwork expectations), department leaders must make efforts to build good relationships with other departments. Department collaborations can be seen by efficient processes with limited gridlocks.

8. *Was there a high level of retention?* Retaining employees is one of the factors that shows a great place to work. Simply, if employees are happy working at their current organization, then they are likely to stay with the organization. Typically, human resources departments maintain an employee retention metric, which upon request is usually shared with the leaders of the organization. This metric is designed to measure employee volunteer resignations during certain specific times, whether it be monthly and/or yearly. If the percentage is low, such as 20 percent or lower, then the retention of 80 percent or more is considered satisfactory with most organizations.

9. *Did the leaders communicate their strategies behind the organizational and/or team objectives with the employees?* Good communication and transparency throughout organizations have always contributed to great places of work. Informed staff are usually more productive, given the fact that, if they understand the rationale behind the objectives, they will likely find ways to help meet these objectives.

10. *Were there leadership accountabilities on behalf of the team?* There will be times when teams will not meet expectations, and while there will be various reasons for it, the leader of that team must always take responsibility for the actions of his or her team. It is part of the reasonability of being a leader, and it would strengthen the leader's credibility.

11. *Did the leader practice fairness and avoid favoring specific staff members?* Favoritism is a conduct that all leaders should avoid because

not only it contradicts fairness, but it also weakens the credibility of leaders. Unfortunately, if a favoritism environment is created by a leader, it will take a conscious effort by the leader to remedy the situation, and it will take a significant amount of time to be accomplished.

12. Lastly, *Did the leader recognize and reward his or her team members for their efforts?* Every great place of work has a method or a program for recognizing and rewarding staff for their efforts. It is another means of saying Thank You, given the fact that without the employees, the teams and organizations would not be successful.

Establishing a great place to work cannot be achieved without the constant effort of great leaders, and such leaders understand that to do it is not a short and random process; in fact, creating a great place to work takes strategy, transparency, patience, and consistency.

Sharing Knowledge With Others

By now, seasoned leaders understand that leadership comes with responsibilities, social consciousness, strong values, and, above all, unconstrained selflessness. Moreover, seasoned leaders should have or are likely to reach the level of expertise in their field, and most (if not all) have the desire to share their knowledge, experiences, and learning lessons throughout their career to those with less knowledge and experience in the field.

On many occasions, knowledge sharing is performed during everyday work, whether it be through coaching, training, and/or through daily interactions. Some leaders began teaching in colleges and/or are giving seminars for various professional associations, while others are publishing articles and books; in addition, some leaders are appearing on podcasts, and some have even created their own podcasts.

However, for some leaders, the greatest challenge is determining the subject matters to share with others that are relevant and important for the current time or, in some cases, the future. For that reason, these leaders have decided to take a comprehensive approach by focusing on three major and broad areas of the discipline that they can share their knowledge with those in the same profession or discipline:

1. *The Foundation of the Discipline*: By focusing on the core of the discipline, leaders are able to teach or reinforce the basics of each topic of the discipline in order for others to continue their development as they reach a higher level of learning. Naturally, this area of edification is for those entry-level professionals who are at the beginning of their profession, or in some cases, for those in the early stage of their profession who never had proper fundamental training.

2. *The Intermediate Level of the Discipline*: At this level, leaders focus on those individuals who are two or three years in their field to help elevate their knowledge to the advanced stages of their profession.

3. *The Advanced Level of the Discipline*: As professionals reach the advanced level of their profession, the seasoned leader will focus their efforts on helping these individuals to reach the level of expertise. This will require either a discussion on strategies, or a profound discussion on each topic, or, on some occasions, both.

Lastly, there are no limits or limited methods for leaders to share their knowledge with others. In fact, throughout time, there have been many conscientious and thoughtful leaders who believed that knowledge should not be hidden, or worse, destroyed; rather knowledge should be passed from one human to another through one generation to the next generation.

Reflections

There will be a time during this final stage of leadership in which leaders will reflect on their career, whether it will be near their retirement period or prior to retirement while developing their successor. Naturally, there will be mixed emotions, with some regrets at certain times, while hopefully, satisfaction at most times.

For those great leaders, looking back at their careers allows them to think of their accomplishments, disappointments, and/or the people that they positively impacted. Some of these great leaders might have created a legacy in which their past efforts have a long-lasting impact on others and/or the organization. Regrettably, these great leaders tend to be far less than those ineffective leaders who either left the organization as failed leaders or maintained their role as unexceptional leaders in the organization, only to create a standard of mediocrity in that organization.

At any point in a leader's career, he or she should think back during the beginning of their leadership career and ask themselves the *Ultimate Question* as to why they decided to enter into a leadership role. Was it for monetary advancements? Was it for professional status and self-image? Was it for commanding authority over others? Was it to make a positive difference to others? Was it to help the organization thrive, so it can maintain its business functions while creating job security for all the employees? Was it to simply create an overall standard of leadership excellence? Or was it because there were so many bad leaders that you (the individual) decided to enter leadership to be part of a positive change by becoming a better leader than the existing or past bad leaders?

How a person answers the Ultimate Question will set the path for his or her entire career in leadership. No bad leader is the same. No effective leader is the same. No style of leadership is the same, and of course, every great leader has made mistakes at some point in their careers.

Leadership is an Evolutionary Process, as much as being a human being that has different stages of his or her life, from early development stages to maturity and hopefully leading to wisdom. To evolve as a leader, it takes several stages with no limited time in each stage. For many, it is foreseeable to spend years developing their fundamental leadership skills simply because it is the most critical stage of leadership. It allows the individual to build a strong leadership foundation before moving forward to the next stage.

Finally, imagine a workplace where the leaders in the organization, from supervisors to CEO, have high regard for their staff. Imagine these leaders leading by example, influence, and empowering their staff, rather than leading by authority, tyranny, micromanagement, and fear. Imagine an organization not only promotes discussion but actually listens to their employees. Imagine an organization that utilizes their employee's ideas and properly rewards them for it. Imagine an organization that has little management–employee relations conflicts. Imagine an organization providing job security for their employees. Imagine a culture in which employees publicly endorse the organization. With great leadership, the imaginative can be achieved, and it will only take one good leader to help start and influence the process of great change.

References

Altawil, S. 2019. *On the Edge of Effectiveness*. 90-Minute Books.

Bass, B. 1981. *Handbook of Leadership*. New York, NY, London, Toronto, Sydney: The Free Press.

Beldoch, M. 1964. "8 Michael Beldoch Sensitivity to Expression of Emotional Meaning in Three Modes of Communication M. Beldoch, 'Sensitivity to Expression of Emotional Meaning in Three Modes of Communication,' in J.R. Davitz et al, The Communication of Emotional." *Social Encounters*, p. 121.

Blake, R.R., J.S. Mouton, L. Barnes, and L. Greiner. 1964. *Breakthrough in Organization Development*. New York, NY: Graduate School of Business Administration, Harvard University.

Burns, J.M. 1978. *Leadership*. Manhattan, New York, NY: Harper & Row.

Carlyle, T. 1869. *Heroes and Hero-Worship* 12. Regent Street, London: Chapman and Hall.

Chard, P. 2013. "Public Persona Matters Most: Accepting Yourself Is the Most Important Step." *Milwaukee Journal Sentinel*. https://archive.jsonline.com/news/health/public-persona-matters-to-most-0s9gmi3-203039951.html/.

Drucker, P. 1954. *The Practice of Management*. New York, NY: Harper& Brothers.

Emeri, P.N. 2022. "Influence of Social Skills on Graduate Employability Among Graduate Workers in Lagos, Nigeria: Sociological Implications." *African Education and Diaspora Studies*, p. 120.

Fiedler, F. 1964. "A Contingency Model of Leadership Effectiveness." In *Advances in Experimental Social Psychology*, pp. 149–190. Philadelphia, PA: Elsevier.

Galton, F. 1891. *Hereditary Genius*. D. Snelling Avenue, Minnesota: Appleton.

Goleman, D. 1996. "Emotional Intelligence. Why It Can Matter More Than IQ." *Learning* 24, no. 6, pp. 49–50.

Grace, M. 2003. "Origins of Leadership: The Etymology of Leadership." *Annual Conference of the International Leadership Association*.

Henman, L. 2011. "Leadership: Theories and Controversies." *Erişim Tarihi* 23, p. 2017.

Hersey, P. and K. Blanchard. 1969. "Life Cycle Theory of Leadership." *Training & Development Journal* 23, pp. 26–34.

Jabli, M. 2022. "Why Cultivating Relationships Is Key to Building Your Business." *Forbes*. www.forbes.com/sites/forbesbusinesscouncil/2022/03/03/why-cultivating-relationships-is-key-to-building-your-business/?sh=5b5f4455746f.

Katz, D. and R. Kahn. 1978. *The Social Psychology of Organizations* 2. New York, NY: Wiley.

Kennedy, J.F. 1961. "Address 'The President and the Press' Before the American Newspaper Publishers Association, New York City. April 27, 1961." *Public Papers of the Presidents of the United States: John F. Kennedy. January 20 to December 31.*

Kotter, J. 1995. *Leading Change: Why Transformation Efforts Fail.* New York, NY: Harvard Business School Publication Corp 73.

Lewin, K. 1947. *Change Management Model.* New York, NY: McGraw Hill.

MacGregor, D. 1960. *The Human Side of Enterprise* 21. New York, NY: McGraw-Hill.

Maslow, A. 1950. *Social Theory of Motivation.* New York, NY: Social Sciences Publishers.

Merchant, R. 2010. "The Role of Career Development in Improving Organizational Effectiveness and Employee Development." *Florida Department of Law Enforcement*, pp. 1–17.

Moldoveanu, M. and D. Narayandas. 2019. "The Future of Leadership Development." *Harvard Business Review* 97, no. 2, pp. 40–48.

Northouse, P. 2021. *Leadership: Theory and Practice.* Teller Road, Newbury Park: SAGE publications.

Obama, B. 2009. "Inaugural Address by President Barack Obama." *The White House: Office of the Press Secretary.*

Organ, C. 2022. "What Are Cross-Functional Teams? Everything You Need to Know." *Forbes Advisor.* www.forbes.com/advisor/business/cross-functional-teams/.

Rani, P. and B. Dhanda. 2018. "The Influence of Caste Soft Skills and Social Skills Development Among Children." *International Journal of Business and General Management (IJBGM)* 7, pp. 95–98.

Salacuse, J.W. 2006. "Leading Leaders: How to Manage the Top Talent in Your Organization." *Ivey Business Journal* 452, p. 50.

Salovey, P. and J. Mayer. 1990. "Emotional Intelligence." *Imagination, Cognition and Personality* 9, no. 3, pp. 185–211.

Skinner, B. 1958. "Reinforcement Today." *American Psychologist* 13, no. 3, p. 94.

Srinivasan, A. and B. Kurey. 2014. "Creating a Culture of Quality." *Harvard Business Review* 92, no. 4, pp. 23–25.

Stogdill, R. 1948. "Personal Factors Associated With Leadership: A Survey of the Literature." *The Journal of Psychology* 25, no. 1, pp. 35–71.

Stogdill, R. and A. Coons. 1957. *Leader Behavior: Its Description and Measurement.* Columbus: Ohio State University, Bureau of Business Research Monograph No. 88.

Tuovila, A. 2022. "Forecasting: What It Is, How It's Used in Business and Investing." *Investopedia.*

Weber, M. 1947. *The Theory of Social and Economic Organization.* Free Press.

Winston, B. 2022. "Relationship of Servant Leadership, Perceived Organizational Support, and Work-Family Conflict With Employee Well-being." *Servant Leadership: Theory & Practice* 9, no. 1, p. 2.

About the Author

Born in the city of Baghdad, **Sam Altawil** came to the United States without any English education. As most immigrants, Sam was able to overcome any challenges and managed to earn his bachelor's degree in social sciences and later accomplished a graduate degree in law, which allowed Sam to enter the field of human resources.

Over 30 years in human resources, 24 of such years were devoted to leadership roles. Sam, as the head of HR, led two outstanding Federally Qualified Health Care Centers, organizations dedicated to serving the underprivileged. Through his leadership, Sam utilized his methodology to improve what once was considered a broken HR department. In 2013, Sam won "best HR practice" in one of the sturdiest Federal audits by the Health Resources and Services Administration (HRSA) department. In 2015 and 2016, Sam and his HR team guided the organization to win "Best Place to Work" by *North Bay Business Journal*, which he repeated in 2023 by winning the Best Place to Work with *San Francisco, Silicon Valley Business Journal*.

Index

OTHER TITLES IN THE HUMAN RESOURCE MANAGEMENT AND ORGANIZATIONAL BEHAVIOR COLLECTION

Michael J. Provitera and Michael Edmondson, Editors

- *11 Secrets of Nonprofit Excellence* by Kathleen Stauffer
- *The Nonprofit Imagineers* by Ben Vorspan
- *At Home With Work* by Nyla Naseer
- *Improv to Improve Your Leadership Team* by Candy Campbell
- *Leadership In Disruptive Times* by Sattar Bawany
- *The Intrapreneurship Formula* by Sandra Lam
- *Navigating Conflict* by Lynne Curry
- *Innovation Soup* by Sanjay Puligadda and Don Waisanen
- *The Aperture for Modern CEOs* by Sylvana Storey
- *The Future of Human Resources* by Tim Baker
- *Change Fatigue Revisited* by Richard Dool and Tahsin I. Alam
- *Championing the Cause of Leadership* by Ted Meyer
- *Embracing Ambiguity* by Michael Edmondson
- *Breaking the Proactive Paradox* by Tim Baker
- *The Modern Trusted Advisor* by Nancy MacKay and Alan Weiss

Concise and Applied Business Books

The Collection listed above is one of 30 business subject collections that Business Expert Press has grown to make BEP a premiere publisher of print and digital books. Our concise and applied books are for...

- Professionals and Practitioners
- Faculty who adopt our books for courses
- Librarians who know that BEP's Digital Libraries are a unique way to offer students ebooks to download, not restricted with any digital rights management
- Executive Training Course Leaders
- Business Seminar Organizers

Business Expert Press books are for anyone who needs to dig deeper on business ideas, goals, and solutions to everyday problems. Whether one print book, one ebook, or buying a digital library of 110 ebooks, we remain the affordable and smart way to be business smart. For more information, please visit www.businessexpertpress.com, or contact sales@businessexpertpress.com.

www.ingramcontent.com/pod-product-compliance
Lightning Source LLC
Chambersburg PA
CBHW061326220326
41599CB00026B/5051